Chaucer the Love Poet

Chaucer the Love Poet

edited by
Jerome Mitchell and William Provost

University of Georgia Press
Athens

Library of Congress Catalog Card Number: 72–97938
International Standard Book Number: 0–8203–0319–4

The University of Georgia Press, Athens 30602

Printed in the United States of America

Contents

Preface

On April 1–2, 1971, a symposium entitled "Chaucer the Love Poet" was held at the University of Georgia under the auspices of the South Atlantic Graduate English cooperative agreement.

The four papers constituting the body of this book are printed here for the first time. They appear essentially in the form in which they were delivered at the symposium, but in each case we have given the author an opportunity to make minor revisions and to add necessary documentation. The panel discussion that follows is a near verbatim transcription of the final session of the symposium. We decided to edit it only slightly, since much of its appeal, we felt, was owing to its informal, off-the-cuff tone. The introduction and the afterword have been especially written for the present book. All quotations from Chaucer follow the standard edition by F. N. Robinson (Boston: Houghton Mifflin Company, 1957).

We would like to express heartfelt thanks to the University of Georgia students, faculty members, and administrators too numerous to be named individually who helped us in various ways in preparing for and managing the symposium. Its resultant success encouraged us to seek a wider audience through publication.

Jerome Mitchell
William Provost

List of Abbreviations

AnM	*Annuale Mediaevale*
ChauR	*The Chaucer Review*
ELH	*Journal of English Literary History*
JEGP	*Journal of English and Germanic Philology*
MLQ	*Modern Language Quarterly*
MLR	*Modern Language Review*
MP	*Modern Philology*
MS	*Mediaeval Studies*
PL	*Patrologia Latina*
SP	*Studies in Philology*

Introduction

The vast outpouring of Chaucer criticism in recent decades makes it almost a moral imperative for the editors of yet one more book on Chaucer to offer some justification for its existence. This is particularly true when the title of the book is *Chaucer the Love Poet*. What more commonplace comment, or commented on topic, can be imagined than love as a feature of Chaucer's poetry? What could be less new and less needed than a collection dealing with so general a theme?

The theme was originally intended for the 1971 SAGE symposium held at the University of Georgia, and it was meant to provide a framework for the conference which would be unifying, but which would not restrict the participants too narrowly. The subject was derived from a remark made some years ago by Norman E. Eliason, who observed that Chaucer is *primarily* a love poet and that no finer love poet has written in the English language.

At the time this seemed an audacious and untenable statement. What about Keats? Shelley? Wyatt? Surrey? Donne? Shakespeare? The statement retains its audacious air (an air, one suspects, that would not be unappreciated by Chaucer himself), but the more one comes to know the work of the first truly great name in the history of English poetry, the more one is convinced that it is wholly justifiable. On occasion one is tempted to make it absolute and unequivocal—something along the lines that Chaucer has no equal as a love poet in English.

This judgment has not often been discussed or specifically commented on in Chaucer criticism. One can easily find critics who speak of love as an element in Chaucer's poetry (indeed, it is hard to find one who does not refer to this in one way or another), or even of Chaucer as a love poet; but one rarely finds criticism that takes as its explicit, basic assumption the idea that Chaucer, in nearly all his writings, is primarily a love poet and a surpassingly excellent love poet. The discussion of this assumption, we believe, deserves presentation to the widest possible audience.

The vast amount of Chaucer criticism makes it impossible for us to present here a comprehensive survey. However, an almost random sampling of the best known critical works can be taken as support for our thesis—that Chaucer has rarely been approached from the viewpoint just mentioned.

Attitudes towards Chaucer's poetry have changed markedly in the nearly six centuries since his death, as Caroline Spurgeon amply demonstrates in *Five Hundred Years of Chaucer Criticism and Allusion*. Her introduction provides a concise summary of these changes. Chaucer's contemporaries and his readers in the fifteenth century were unanimous in their praise, and they universally accepted him as the master poet in English. He was imitated frequently, particularly by his Scottish followers, in the fifteenth and early sixteenth centuries. Approaching the middle of the sixteenth century, praise begins to center around the idea of Chaucer as a satirist and social reformer—particularly in connection with vice among the clergy—and one finds a decreasing appreciation of him as a literary artist. By the end of the century the real decline of Chaucer's reputation has begun, and he becomes a name that, although still frequently referred to, is now normally accompanied by adjectives such as old-fashioned, rude, rough, and obsolete. His language has become foreign and most people simply do not read him. Those who do are put off by his (to them) rough versification and crude stories. There were, of course, always exceptions (Sidney or Spenser, for example, and later Dryden and to some extent Pope), but generally it is this attitude that prevails throughout the seventeenth century and a large part of the eighteenth. It even occurs sporadically in the nineteenth: Byron thought Chaucer obscene, and an anonymous contributor to the *Cornhill Magazine* (March 1877) said that for the most part, "Chaucer's writings are a lackadaisical exaggeration of one feeling—Love, and . . . in them the passion is taken in its weakest, vainest form of sentimentality. He is, and for ever will remain, the chief erotic poet of our language." (This, we suppose, might be taken as a sort of left-handed support for our current thesis.)

Though judgments of this kind can thus be found well into the nineteenth century, the turning point for Chaucer's literary reputation is placed much earlier, in Dryden's famous preface to *Fables Ancient and Modern*. This perceptive and cogent appraisal recognized, described, and defended Chaucer's genius, and the trend it began is still in progress. It grows throughout the eighteenth century and reaches one of its high points in the great rush of admiration that is the typical attitude of most Romantic and Victorian readers. The trend develops in a parallel way into the tradition of modern scholarly criticism, with its specific roots in Tyrwhitt's edition of the *Canterbury Tales* in 1775 and the founding of the Chaucer Society in 1868.

Miss Spurgeon says that the adjectives most frequently and typically applied to Chaucer during these five hundred years are eloquent, moral, learned, jovial, and facetious. For the modern reader several additional attributes are normally associated with Chaucer, including sanity, realism, and, what is more pertinent to our present concern, love. As we begin looking at contemporary scholarship, we see that that attribute still has not been treated in a broad and comprehensive manner. In this century as in the past, most criticism has concentrated on other attributes, or if it has dealt with love, it has done so in a limited way.

Our sampling can appropriately begin with George Lyman Kittredge. In his best known and most influential article Kittredge formulated the Marriage Group theory, which, though obviously concerned with love (or in some cases the lack of it), treats it in only a limited way. Throughout his criticism Kittredge was concerned not so much with Chaucer as a poet of love, but as a poet of humanity. Such statements as "Chaucer's specialty was mankind" or "Next to Shakespeare, Chaucer is the greatest delineator of character in our literature"[1] are indicative of Kittredge's central thesis. Presumably Kittredge meant to include love as one feature of Chaucer's humanity, but he makes relatively few direct references to this feature. He does say, for example, that in the so-called French period Chaucer "was, to all intents and purposes, a French love-poet writing (so it happened) in the English language" (p. 26), and of *Troilus* he admits unhesitatingly that "the subject was to be love" (p. 109), but such remarks hardly constitute a comprehensive or detailed treatment of love in Chaucer.

A similar situation exists in the scholarship of Robert Kilburn

---

1. *Chaucer and His Poetry* (Cambridge: Harvard University Press, 1915), pp. 9, 29.

Root, who also sees as Chaucer's primary attribute his overall sanity and broad point of view: "With the possible exception of Shakespeare, there is no English poet of power even commensurate with Chaucer's, who is so eminently sane." Root sees in Chaucer a great talent for irony and humor, calling his a "spirit of health and free-hearted joy."[2] He sees as the basic characteristic of *Troilus and Criseyde* not that it is a great love poem, but that it is a poem of wisdom and irony: "It is in this spirit of a wise and thoughtful irony that Chaucer has conceived and executed his poem, a spirit poles asunder from the tender sentiment and ardent passion which inform the *Filostrato*."[3] When he does discuss love in Chaucer, it is frequently in relation to some other subject. In discussing the Franklin's Tale, for example, Root says, "Beautiful as is this picture of married love, Chaucer has taken care that it shall not become sentimental, by touching it here and there with his own peculiar humor."[4]

John Livingston Lowes similarly speaks of Chaucer as a poet of sanity, of life, of humor, rather than as a poet of love. He can say of *Troilus and Criseyde* that it is one of the very great and beautiful poems of the world and that Books II and III—the central part of the love story proper—are the heart of the poem,[5] but he sees its real topic as its ironical view of life, not its depiction of love. Chaucer "has depicted, with what he must have known to be almost supreme art, the tragic irony of life" (p. 154). Perhaps the following could serve as Lowes's summary statement on Chaucer: "And Chaucer's individual, peculiar quality lies in large measure in that eager appetence of his for life, to which nothing was common or unclean" (p. 193). One is reminded of Dryden's famous statement (which Lowes quotes with approval): "He is a perpetual fountain of good sense."

Percy Van Dyke Shelly is perhaps the most notable exception to the general tendency we have been observing. Shelly says of Chaucer that "until he did the *Canterbury Tales* [he] wrote virtually nothing but poems dealing in one way or another with the subject of love." He very definitely characterizes Chaucer as a

2. *The Poetry of Chaucer* (Boston: Houghton Mifflin, 1906), pp. 43, 150.
3. *The Book of Troilus and Criseyde* (Princeton: Princeton University Press, 1926), p. xlix.
4. *The Poetry of Chaucer*, p. 275.
5. *Geoffrey Chaucer* (Oxford: Clarendon Press, 1934), pp. 133–137.

love poet: "So far from being a moral, religious, philosophical, or edifying poet, he deliberately made himself a love poet and thought of and described himself as a love poet."[6] Shelly's omission of the *Canterbury Tales* from what he considers to be Chaucer's love poetry is an indication that there are still some important differences between his approach and the one we are suggesting. In studying Chaucer as a love poet it seems neither necessary nor desirable to omit what many consider his finest work, and what is certainly his best known and most ambitious. Shelly treats love in a restricted way, dealing primarily with what we might term "romantic love." He is not, furthermore, as widely read or as important a critic of Chaucer as the others mentioned. His approach is closer to appreciation than to true criticism, and his atypical stance regarding love as one of Chaucer's basic themes has not been a part of the main development of such criticism.

C. S. Lewis, like Shelly, would seem to be dealing specifically with Chaucer as a love poet, but his work cannot be said to constitute a comprehensive treatment of this idea. Lewis's basic contention is that Chaucer wrote within a particular mode and a particular convention—the mode of allegory and the convention of courtly love. He thus does not refer to Chaucer simply as a love poet, but says instead that "Chaucer is a poet of courtly love."[7] It is interesting that Lewis also excludes the *Canterbury Tales* from the main body of Chaucer's love poetry, and for essentially the same reason as did Shelly—the *Tales* do not treat the kind of love with which he is concerned. Referring to *Troilus and Criseyde*, Lewis says that it "is the consummation, not the abandonment, of his labors as a poet of *courtly* love" (p.176; italics ours). Lewis's ultimate view of Chaucer is not as our chief love poet, but as "our supreme poet of happiness" (p.197).

The three final critics to be mentioned are also concerned with love in Chaucer, and in one way or another with courtly love. Thomas A. Kirby, D. W. Robertson, Jr., and E. Talbot Donaldson are all well aware of the fact that love is an important feature of Chaucer's poetry. Kirby, for example, has dealt in great detail with the theme of courtly love as it appears in *Troilus and*

6. *The Living Chaucer* (Philadelphia: University of Pennsylvania Press, 1940), pp. 2, 12.
7. *The Allegory of Love* (Oxford: Oxford University Press, 1936), p.161.

Criseyde,[8] and he has provided a number of excellent insights, such as his comparison of Troilus and Diomede as lovers. His work, however, like that of Shelly and Lewis, is tied to a specific type of love and does not purport to examine that broader question which the editors of this book believe is framed in the pages that follow.

Robertson also deals with love in a limited way. In his most influential work, *A Preface to Chaucer: Studies in Medieval Perspectives*,[9] he deals with mode and theme, the mode again being allegory (though different in a number of respects from that discussed by Lewis) and the theme love. Robertson's provocative notions as to *how* medieval literature means and must be read go hand in hand with his ideas about the sort of love Chaucer and other medieval writers were concerned with. He denies the existence of the conventions of courtly love—be they historical or merely literary—and talks instead of *caritas* and *cupiditas*, or more correctly the relations between the two. Teaching the proper relation between them, according to Robertson, is the real purpose of any serious work of medieval literature. Robertson has had enormous influence on the study and criticism of Chaucer and on the question of love in Chaucer. But there is more to be said.

Donaldson too has pointed out the dangerous and probably fallacious assumptions about "courtly love" that are routinely made by many contemporary scholars.[10] He sees a basic morality in Chaucer—though not one based, as Robertson would have it, entirely on an Augustinian *caritas–cupiditas* hierarchy—and is certainly aware that love is an important element in his poetry. He says, for example, that romantic love, both as "a theme and an attitude," is treated with grandeur in *Troilus and Criseyde*.[11] Courtly love is certainly not the only kind that can be found in Chaucer, and we owe much to Robertson and Donaldson for their warnings. In neither of them, however, have we found the broad and comprehensive examination of love in Chaucer which ought to exist.

8. *Chaucer's "Troilus": A Study in Courtly Love* (Baton Rouge: Louisiana State University Press, 1940).

9. Princeton: Princeton University Press, 1962.

10. "The Myth of Courtly Love," in *Speaking of Chaucer* (New York: Norton, 1970), pp. 154–163.

11. *Chaucer's Poetry: An Anthology for the Modern Reader* (New York: Ronald Press, 1958), p. 965.

It is exactly such an examination that we believe this book can inaugurate. The time has come—and it is a particularly appropriate time—to approach Chaucer's work from the assumption that he is primarily a love poet and a surpassingly excellent one. Scholars have not consistently done this, although Chaucer's contemporaries seem to have accepted the assumption unreservedly. In the *Testament of Love* (1387) Thomas Usk has the goddess of Love herself refer to Chaucer as "myne owne trewe seruaunt / the noble philosophical poete / in Englissh whiche evermore him besyeth and trauayleth right sore my name to encrease." John Gower, in the first version of the *Confessio Amantis*, has Venus say,

> And gret wel Chaucer whan ye mete,
> As mi disciple and mi poete . . .
> Whereof to him in special
> Aboue alle othre I am most holde.

As C. S. Lewis has said of such early commentaries, "There is something to be said for them. . . . If they all took Chaucer's love poetry *au grand serieux*, it is overwhelmingly probable that Chaucer himself did the same."[12] It is time that we do so too.

We are today very strongly attracted, engrossed, and puzzled by the idea of love. Think of a few more or less recent titles that use the word: *The Love Machine, Love Story, The Art of Loving, Love in the Ruins.* . . . Such a list could be extended considerably, but these four sufficiently document the confusion we seem to have about the word and the concept behind it. Chaucer was neither uncertain nor confused about love, and this alone makes him a particularly refreshing, interesting, and enlightening poet for the modern reader.

Questions involving the relationship between artist or critic and the particular culture which produces him, and the degree to which the human heart is really changeable, are indeed difficult, but this much at least seems axiomatic: cultural perspectives and critical approaches change, but the changes need not be seen as negating or detracting from what has been said earlier. The classics of criticism remain; but leaving these aside, it is the job of

12. *The Allegory of Love*, p. 163.

each new generation of critics to read English literature and to express its perception of that literature in valid contemporary language.

The approach of the present book is that of reading Chaucer as a love poet—not a poet of courtly love, romantic love, Boethian love, physical love, divine love, or any other particular kind of love—but simply as a love poet.[13] We believe that love, in the broadest and most inclusive sense of the word, was Chaucer's deepest and most passionate interest and his all but invariable topic. He was certainly a poet of humanity, of sanity, of irony, and of humor, but to say that he was a poet of love includes all these and more. He gives us explicit notice of the wide range of his interest in love. If we can momentarily set aside the problems involving the persona and the proper location of ironic distance, we see that in a limited yet real sense it is the same poet who responds to the wonder of a night of sexual intercourse with the line "Why nad I swich oon with my soule ybought" and to the wonder of God's love with the line "So make us, Jesus, for thi mercy digne." We are on dangerous ground if we totally deny validity to one or the other of these responses. And we need not do so if we are willing to talk in an unreserved and unrestricted way about Chaucer the love poet.

Taken together, the four papers and the panel discussion that form the main portion of this book constitute such an unreserved and unrestricted discussion—from the general approaches of Professors Eliason and Reiss to the more specific of Professors Kaske and Wimsatt, from "ordinary" love to parodic love to erotic love, from the Canticle of Canticles to Ann Landers. We believe the discussion suggests an approach that is useful for readers and critics, and we wish to present it to a larger audience than was able to attend the symposium itself.

William Provost

13. Many scholarly works, books and articles, exist which are devoted to particular features of Chaucer's works, but which also treat, at least in passing, this very topic. Taken individually, each of the four papers here presented treats a specific feature of Chaucer's artistry. Taken collectively, we believe that a more inclusive and ultimately more important topic is suggested.

Chaucer the Love Poet

The fact that Chaucer is a love poet, the first of any consequence in English and one of the finest who ever wrote, would seem too obvious to be worth mentioning were it not for the scant recognition it receives today. Aside from *Troilus and Criseyde* where it is inescapable, the excellence of his love poetry is now usually overlooked. One reason, I think, is that we ignore what is really best there, and the other is that we have grown so accustomed to a different mode of love poetry that his fails to impress us. Because he does not rhapsodize about love, we are inclined to dismiss his as not being love poetry at all. Even *Troilus* does not escape this fate, being egregiously mislabeled as our first psychological novel or, less foolishly but quite as mischievously, subjected to critical scrutiny which disregards the fact that it is the greatest love poem in the language.

Before proceeding further, I had best say what I mean by the term. A love poem, I take it, is one which has something interesting to say about love and says it well. As a definition this would seem innocuous enough to avoid needless argument and yet it is strict enough to rule out many poems that are not worth bothering about—including some of Chaucer's.

There remains the crux, the word *love* and the particular sense to be given it here. One way of handling the matter would be to take into account all the various senses it has in the more than fourteen hundred times Chaucer uses the word, but the result would not be very satisfactory, leaving us to conclude with Chaucer that "what love is, thou canst not seen ne gesse." The other way, which I shall adopt, is to single out for special attention one particular sense—the sense which Webster's defines as the "tender and passionate affection for one of the opposite sex"—for this is not only the most common one today and the one which most naturally comes to mind when we speak of love poetry but it is also the most rewarding one when we give serious consideration to Chaucer as a love poet.

This particular kind of love—which for want of anything better I shall label "ordinary love"—is, to be sure, not the only kind Chaucer writes about. Among these other kinds, only four require notice: allegorical, courtly, philosophic, and Christian love. If they had not already had a vast amount of attention or if any of them were of vital significance in Chaucer's love poetry, I would not deal with them as perfunctorily as I propose to do here.

By allegorical love I mean the kind depicted more fully and for Chaucer more memorably in the *Romance of the Rose* than in any other of his *olde bokes* where he claimed to have learned about love. From the *Romance*, unfortunately, he learned how to write about love in a way that prevented him from saying anything significant about it. Love was depicted there as a dream experience, requiring an account both of how the poet came to have his dream and of what he dreamt. In Chaucer's hands neither the preliminaries to the dream nor the dream itself proved successful, the one leading him astray and the other leading nowhere.

To the preliminary business, which in the *Romance* was briefly disposed of, Chaucer could make additions and did—prolonging the account of how he got to sleep, for example, or speculating about the causes of dreams and their significance. However delightful all this may be, it is only introductory, and by dwelling upon it at length Chaucer made the introduction inordinately long, producing the lopsided structure which mars all his dream-vision poems.

The dream, as recounted in the *Romance*, is about a young man's efforts to pluck a rosebud growing in a garden and about the help afforded him by the god of love and his retinue and the hindrance afforded by the god of love's enemies. This allegorical method of treating love is both charming and perceptive. Personifying the passion and its operation in this way makes it easier to expound the complex motives involved and makes it possible to do so circumspectly. Instead of bluntly saying what a young man wants, it can be put fancifully, delicately, and yet clearly enough. No one who reads the *Romance* can fail to grasp that it is not just a rosebud that the young man wants to pluck—no one at least with wit enough to realize that the *Romance of the Rose* is something other than a horticultural treatise.

To such love allegory addition or alteration was impossible—or so Chaucer evidently believed. He kept the god of love unchanged, always depicting him in the same way as in the *Romance*. To equip him with a sword rather than a bow was unthinkable, and to add any arrows to his quiver was unnecessary. And this holds true of Venus and the other pagan deities who, like the contending factions in the *Romance*, had long been established as conventional love symbols. Chaucer could maneuver them into odd situations, but he could or would not alter their allegorical significance. Hence about allegorical love, though he may and occasionally does employ it more deftly than it had been before, Chaucer certainly says nothing new.

Four of his major works, the *Book of the Duchess*, the *House of Fame*, the *Parliament of Fowls*, and the *Legend of Good Women*—all of them early save perhaps the last—are dream-vision poems with lavish introductions leading up to the dream but utilizing love allegory only sporadically. The meaning and merit of these poems have been endlessly discussed but with curiously inconclusive results. Perhaps some of our doubts might be dispelled by asking whether they are love poems and answering not by tacitly assuming that they are, but by subjecting them to the test of whether they have anything interesting to say about love.

Two obviously do not pass the test, for neither the *Legend of Good Women* nor the *Book of the Duchess* is concerned with love at all. The concern of the latter is not love but, as the poem is now invariably construed, the loss of a loved one, more particularly the loss suffered by John of Gaunt at the death of his wife Blanche. But if the poem is indeed an elegy lamenting her death or a funerary poem commemorating it, the very least we might expect there is a sincere and moving tribute to Blanche and a satisfying consolation for her husband, both of whom were Chaucer's friends and benefactors. The expectation is not fulfilled. Chaucer even fails to make clear the basic fact that it is about Blanche until, two-thirds of the way through, he coyly reveals it in a pun and never reveals the name of her bereaved husband. About other facts Chaucer is simply wrong, such as John's age, said to be twenty-four whereas it actually was twenty-nine at the time of his wife's death. Above all, however, it is the tone of the whole thing that is utterly and inexplicably wrong, for from beginning to end there are little touches of frivolity that give it a light-hearted air totally unsuitable for such a poem. As an elegy it is the oddest if not the worst ever written. Our choice is either to admit this and explain as best we can how and why Chaucer botched it so badly or to seek some other interpretation of the poem which will accord with or mitigate its apparent flaws.

The *Legend of Good Women* is not concerned with love either. The nine legends contained there are about women who fared badly at the hands of men, some being seduced, some raped, some deserted, and some killing themselves. Since no attempt is made to explain their misfortunes, none of these good women elicit any real sympathy nor the legends any critical concern. Why Chaucer never completed the work, writing all of the nineteen or twenty legends he once planned to, is less remarkable than why he persisted long enough to write the nine he did. Critical concern is now confined to the Prologue, a work to which Chaucer apparently gave exceptional care. Our only concern here is to note that, though the whole Prologue deals with love allegory in the sense that the god of love and his retinue are out in full force there, the allegory has no significance. Its sole function is to bring the trumped-up charge against Chaucer that he had violated the laws of this god and to fix the penalty for this, Chaucer being doomed to write the legends which follow. Thus, however admirably the Prologue succeeds in introducing the legends, it is clearly not a love poem nor was it intended to be.

Both the *House of Fame* and the *Parliament of Fowls* pass the test of having something interesting to say but in neither is it quite about love. The concern of the *House of Fame* is not love but love tidings, more particularly a certain tiding or rumor which obviously was about to be divulged by some "man of gret auctoritee" just as the poem abruptly breaks off, leaving the rumor undisclosed. This unfinished ending, surely the crux in interpreting the poem aright, suggests what Chaucer's purpose was. What he wanted to do—or so it seems to me—was to squelch this particular rumor and hence of course he refrained from recounting it, using the simple ruse of leaving the poem unfinished and stopping at the precise point where he did. But he also needed to demonstrate that the rumor was false, doing so not by solemn or vociferous denial but by laughing it to scorn. How he did so and how adroitly he managed it I shall not go into here, for I have set this forth fully enough in my book *The Language of Chaucer's Poetry*. Here I shall merely point out that in squelching the rumor as effectively as he did—leaving us still in the dark today about who was involved in this amatory scandal—Chaucer was evidently too adroit. At any rate his adroitness has eluded critics of the poem who, though managing to find all sorts of praiseworthy solemnity there about love and other serious matters, wind up admitting that they really can make nothing of the poem.

The *Parliament of Fowls* has fared much the same way at the hands of modern critics, who find an astonishing amount of profundity about love in general there. Instead of love in general, I believe that the poem deals with a specific love problem, the problem of getting a mate, traditionally the special concern on Saint Valentine's day, the occasion of the poem. And as a Valentine day poem, it is sheer delight, for it concentrates solely on this problem and, instead of examining it solemnly, treats it fancifully. The fancy takes two turns. The one imagines what would happen if mating were made a matter of parliamentary business, debated there by politicians who in weighing the pros and cons of the issue could only have made a mess of the problem and a hash of the poem, converting it into satire or burlesque. This disastrous effect, however, is forestalled by the other turn of the fancy, whereby the parliament is imagined as composed of birds, who can argue the matter with birdlike logic and fervor, the ducks applying their brains to it and the turtledoves their sentimentality. And it is thus that the problem is solved to everyone's satisfaction, all the birds getting their mates and blissfully flying off singing their praise of Saint Valentine—all except a luckless foursome. The foursome includes a female eagle who, given her choice of three worthy and devoted suitors, can't make up her mind and is given a year's reprieve to ponder the matter. What eventually happened—whether the three male eagles used the time to press on with their suit or to shop around elsewhere and whether the female remained adamantly demure and coy—we are not told. Nor do we care in the least, for we too join in the joyous song at the end of the poem. Thus although love, as Chaucer reminds us at the beginning of the poem, is a perplexing matter involving vast effort and pain, even its most crucial and troublesome business, getting a mate, can be viewed as a joyous affair.

If allegorical love, because of its rigid conventions, constrained Chaucer from saying anything new about love, courtly love prevented him from saying anything significant about it. However courtly love should be defined—a moot question now that its codifiers, from Andreas Capellanus in the thirteenth century to C. S. Lewis in the twentieth, have been rejected—two of its special characteristics are worth attention. One of them, the idealization of love, has had a great deal; the other, its setting, has not. By setting I do not mean merely its courtly scene or the dress, the manners, and the customs described there but rather the heightened way in which all this was done and the pomp and ceremony ascribed to it. This rich setting was and still remains one of the chief attractions of courtly love literature. Regardless of who challenges whom there, or who wins the combat or the girl, or however she is won or lost, it is the glitter, the color, the sound, and the panoply which—whether in conformity with the realities of the time or not—have always provided much of its delight. But, what is more to the point, it is this which shapes the kind of love portrayed there. Love in a castle is not quite the same as in a cottage.

The idealization which this kind of love involved, however, is something else. Even to a cottage dweller, a castle is at least imaginable. But when the love of a man and woman is so etherealized that he isn't sure whether she is a woman or a goddess and she is too demure to set him straight about it, then obviously their love is of an altogether different kind from that of concern to all cottage dwellers and, I suspect, most castle dwellers too. Idealized love like this becomes a pretty but idle fancy, incapable of eliciting thought and unlikely to arouse interest and certainly not to sustain it.

Both of these characteristics are amply displayed in the Knight's Tale, where the elaborate setting gives it the showy qualities that Chaucer evidently thought suitable for the opening tale of the Canterbury collection but the idealized love portrayed there deprives it of any worth as a love poem or any interest even as a love story. The rival claims of Palamon and Arcite, two equally hare-brained young men, for the hand of Emily, possibly the most mindless heroine in all literature, the preposterous series of events which culminate in the winning of the girl, and the final outcome, where the winner loses her by being unceremoniously pitched off his horse to his death and the loser wins her by the autocratic decree of the ruler of the realm, constitute a story too fatuous for any serious consideration. Critics however are almost unanimously of the opposite opinion, maintaining that the outcome poses a profound philosophical problem and scratching their heads for a profound solution of it, or construing the whole poem in an even weightier way by insisting that its real concern is not the story but the even more profound philosophical problem of universal order posed, they insist, throughout the work.

Whatever the proper critical assessment of the Knight's Tale may be, the work provides an excellent opportunity for appraising the merits and weaknesses of courtly love as Chaucer views and exploits it there. After the Knight's Tale he continued to write about courtly love but never again constructed a whole work on or around it. Some of his works and even the Knight's Tale itself have been construed as repudiations of courtly love, but this is wrong, I think. Chaucer never holds the concept up to scorn. When he mocks it, as he does occasionally elsewhere, the mockery is directed at some particular manifestation or misapplication of it, usually by showing the absurdity when misemployed by someone not to the manner born. Chaucer was neither an enemy nor a champion of courtly love. With him the concept remained unchallenged, serviceable for dealing with love elegantly and useless for dealing with it seriously.

Unchanged at Chaucer's hands also was philosophical love—the kind praised and expounded from antiquity down through the Middle Ages as the force which controls the order of the whole universe and guarantees its continuity. Its primary exponent, so far as Chaucer is concerned, was Boethius, his favorite philosopher and the direct or indirect source of nearly all of his more profound ideas. Of concern to us here is not the origin or transmission of this philosophical conception of love but simply the fact that Chaucer invokes it repeatedly but utilizes it in two quite different ways—to give an air of weightiness to works like the Knight's Tale, which really doesn't need it and can hardly sustain it, or to give depth to works like *Troilus*, where it is of inestimable help in showing that the love there is something more than mere passion.

Closely allied to philosophical love is Christian love, which in its highest sense is the concept that God is love, a concept which Chaucer of course was content to accept and undisposed to modify. He also accepted the Christian doctrine that carnal love

is sin, letting the Parson expound it soberly and uncompromising-
ly. And the Parson does so, pointing out for example that sexual
intercourse, even in marriage when indulged in for any reason
other than procreation, is wrong. Chaucer also lets the Wife of
Bath expound this uncomfortable doctrine and grapple with the
delicate distinction between intercourse for the sake of procreation or fun. And her way of expounding it is neither sober nor
uncompromising, for she sums it all up in her heartfelt lament,
"Allas! allas! that evere love was synne!" Whether Chaucer himself leaned more to the Wife's view than to the Parson's may be
questionable, but his acceptance of the doctrine is not, for he
acknowledges it clearly at the end of both *Troilus* and the *Canterbury Tales.*

Both passages have caused much trouble for critics. Just how
or if the conclusion of *Troilus* is artistically justifiable lies beyond
our concern here, which is solely with the fact that Chaucer
unmistakably repudiates carnal love there, the very kind he had
portrayed sympathetically throughout the poem. Much the same
holds true of the conclusion of the *Canterbury Tales*, where again
we need only note here that Chaucer asks Christ's mercy for
writing *Troilus* as well as those "tales of Caunterbury . . . that
sownen into synne." In not specifying which tales he had in mind,
it was surely not Chaucer's intention to puzzle either God or us.
The only puzzle there is why some modern critics deny the clear
meaning of the remark by insisting that none of the tales of the
Canterbury collection are really sinful at all. The entire work,
they maintain, is moral since its underlying and unifying theme
is love in the most extensive Christian sense of *caritas*, or love of
God and of one's fellow men, a sense made even more extensive
by the inclusion of its direct opposite *cupiditas*, or love of self. As
a means of clarification these opposites were often joined together in the Middle Ages. Chaucer himself uses the method in the
Parson's Tale, where the seven deadly sins are matched up with
their contrasting virtues. But though sin and virtue or *caritas* and
cupiditas might thus be combined, they were never confused.
Only a rogue would have confused them deliberately and only a
fool could have blurred the distinction. And in none of his writings is Chaucer a fool or a rogue, befuddled about what he means
or trying to befuddle us about it.

My perfunctory treatment of these four kinds of love—Christian, philosophic, courtly, and allegorical—and my peremptory dismissal of them may readily be misunderstood. My intention has not been to denigrate them, to deny their validity, or to belittle scholarly concern about them. These concepts of love or ways of treating it were commonplace in Chaucer's day, and that is obviously why he made extensive use of them. Without some knowledge of all four, we cannot understand Chaucer's poetry. But to appreciate his love poetry, which is anything but commonplace, we must not confine our attention to them, for its concern is love of an altogether different kind—ordinary love, as I have proposed calling it. Distinguishing, as I do, between ordinary love and the four other kinds may seem to be quite arbitrary, and indeed it is. But it is no more arbitrary than distinguishing among the other four, which, though usually combined in one way or another by Chaucer, are nonetheless separated by critics and treated separately.

Disposing of these four kinds of love, as I am doing here, and denying that the poems of Chaucer which are concerned only with one or another of these are really love poems, may seem to rob him of any real claim to being a love poet at all. Far from damaging his claim, however, it enhances it. The recognition that love is merely the topic but not the true concern of some of Chaucer's poems should have the salutary effect of shifting critical attention from their substance, which doesn't merit it, to their technique, which does. If, as I have been maintaining, what Chaucer says about any of these conventional kinds of love is essentially nothing more than what others had said before, then all that really matters there is the way he says it. And if we will attend to such poems accordingly, we can get at the things of consequence there, detecting for example his success with technique in the *House of Fame* and the *Parliament of Fowls* and his failure with it in the *Book of the Duchess* and the Knight's Tale. But if we look squint-eyed at them, seeking for profound ideas about love in the *Parliament* for example but not finding them and yet refusing to admit it, and also seeking for his success in expressing these undiscoverable ideas, the result is the kind of criticism we now have—an endless and fruitless controversy over issues too ill-defined ever to be resolvable.

My insistence upon the primary importance of ordinary love in Chaucer may, I realize, seem both simple-minded and anachronistic. Love, as we are constantly reminded by Chaucer scholars, was not viewed in the fourteenth century in the same way as it is today. Nothing could be truer or less in need of reminder. We are kept constantly aware of the differences by the strange love conventions encountered on almost every page of Chaucer—conventions which in the course of time have inevitably changed. But this, as Chaucer points out, matters very little:

> Ye knowe ek that in forme of speche is chaunge
> Withinne a thousand yeer, and wordes tho
> That hadden pris, now wonder nyce and straunge
> Us thinketh hem, and yet thei spake hem so,
> And spedde as wel in love as men now do;
> Ek for to wynnen love in sondry ages,
> In sondry londes, sondry ben usages. (*Troilus and Criseyde*, II, 22–28)

Beneath the "sundry usages," varying from place to place and time to time, there is, as he tells us, a changeless concern about love. This concern, obviously shared by people in the fourteenth century, is quite as obviously shared by us today. Then as now there existed the "tender and passionate affection for one of the opposite sex," and it was this concept of love that most people then were primarily interested in. There were exceptions, to be sure—the Parson, for example—but not Chaucer. If we have doubts about this, we need only look to him, for he shows us that it is true.

He also shows us, if we don't already know it, that this concept of love is anything but simple-minded. At any rate he did not find it so, declaring

> that my felynge
> Astonyeth with his [i.e., love's] wonderful werkynge
> So sore, iwis, that whan I on hym thynke,
> Nat wot I wel wher that I flete or synke. (*Parliament of Fowls*, ll. 4–7)

And if we are honest enough to admit it, we too are still astonished and perplexed by such love. Why this ordinary kind of love is neglected in modern Chaucerian criticism is hard to say.

Possibly it is because it seems simple-minded and self-evident or because scholars are skittish about discussing it or, more plausibly, it is because of their preoccupation with the other kinds of love which now seem strange and therefore require elaborate elucidation.

It is about ordinary love that Chaucer has something interesting to say and says it well. This holds true, I believe, of only three of his major poems—*Troilus* certainly and also the tales of the Wife of Bath and the Franklin. But besides these complete poems, there are many passages, scattered throughout the rest of his work, of which it holds true as well. One brief example may suffice here. In the Nun's Priest's Tale Chaunticleer, a rooster wanting to butter up his mate Pertelote and knowing she is ignorant of Latin, declares, "In principio, / Mulier est hominis confusio," following it up immediately with the remark, "Madame, the sentence of this Latyn is, / 'Womman is mannes joye and al his blis.' " Thus in only three lines Chaucer manages to compress not only a little joke and a stinging jab at masculine arrogance but also to express trenchantly the simple but profound truth that woman is the source of all man's bliss as well as his confusion—a truth which when explored fully, as it was in *Troilus*, required five long books. In assessing Chaucer's love poetry it is not to his love poems alone that we must look, for we must also take into account the many scattered comments like Chaunticleer's.

What Chaucer says there about this kind of love would seem to merit careful consideration, especially at a time like ours, when to judge by the continued popularity of Ann Landers and the current best-seller ratings of books like *Everything You Always Wanted to Know About Sex*, the subject obviously is of engrossing interest to millions. Instead of an exhaustive analysis, I shall merely list some of Chaucer's ideas about it: (1) Such love is inspired not by wealth, looks, or social position but by character; (2) Sexual gratification is not its sole objective; (3) Nor, except in fiction, is marriage its final culmination; (4) Without marriage it can be just as deep and sincere as within; (5) Within marriage, affection must be supplemented by patience and mutual tolerance; (6) The question of who is to be boss is, in literature though perhaps not always in life, merely a joking matter; (7) Although such love may endure until death, it is ephemeral nonetheless—as ephemeral as life itself.

None of these ideas may be particularly profound and certainly none are novel, nor were they in Chaucer's day. But they are sound—as sound today, I believe, as they were then. To assert this is of course heresy now, for it is contrary to the dogma proclaimed by our twentieth-century twin goddesses of wisdom who preside over the realms of psychology and sociology and in whom all but simple-minded folk now put their faith. But even though we cannot wholeheartedly subscribe to Chaucer's views about love, we are not compelled to reject them completely. Right or wrong, they are put much too persuasively to be shunted aside as the notions of a funny old fogy who lived too long ago to benefit from the insights of Freud and his followers and Kinsey and his updaters.

Chaucer's persuasiveness stems from several things. One is that he seems to speak with the voice of experience. To be sure, he claims not to, frequently denying any firsthand knowledge of love or any luck with it either—an amusing dodge that took no one in at the time, least of all his wife, I suspect—and one which misleads no one today. Whatever his actual experience, he manages to convey the impression that he knew what he was writing about.

Another is that he writes honestly about love, not pretending for example that sexual intercourse isn't fun nor denying that, because it may relieve nervous tension or because a high percentage of people indulge in it, it is a sin. Nor is he content with the foolish assumption that love is inimical to thinking. He lets Criseyde think. Even when on the verge of falling in love, she proves capable of weighing the issue that every woman faces—save utterly mindless ones like Emily or merely amorous ones like the heroines of Chaucer's fabliaux—when about to give up the security of loneliness in favor of the uncertainty of love. This is, I suppose, what another of our current best-sellers, *Sex and the Single Girl*, is all about. I prefer to read the Chaucerian version, feeling assured that in *Troilus* the whole problem is explored more deeply and honestly. Honesty about love makes for complexity, and nowhere in Chaucer is this more apparent than in his portrayal of Criseyde. Our concern here is not the complexity of her character but one facet of it which is often misunderstood. Chaucer, by endowing her with a mind and revealing how well she could use it, exposed her to the charge that she is calculating and, by endowing her with passion and revealing her delight with its gratification, to the charge that she is wanton. The possession of a mind, I should think, is hardly reprehensible and, however reprehensible her passion no doubt was in the eyes of the Parson, it cannot be condemned as a falsification of human nature. The trouble with Criseyde is that Chaucer made a woman of her, not a goddess, fascinating for her flaws and lovable in spite of them.

A third basis for Chaucer's persuasiveness is that his views about love are sensible, and seem so even today. This quality, long ascribed to Chaucer and singled out for special praise by Dryden, who called him "a perpetual fountain of good sense," is now out of favor with most critics, who are disposed to disdain or deny it. Even those who vehemently protest against viewing Chaucer's work through twentieth-century eyes or judging medieval love by modern romantic standards share this curious contemporary bias against common sense in literature. A case in point is the Franklin's Tale, a story about an admirable young married couple. The tale is now often held up to scorn and its morality denounced as false or banal. Critical ire is directed particularly at the little homily on love and marriage, near the beginning of the poem, which I cite here in abridged form:

> Love wol nat been constreyned by maistrye.
> Whan maistrie comth, the God of Love anon
> Beteth his wynges, and farewel, he is gon!
> Love is a thyng as any spirit free. . . .
> Pacience is an heigh vertu. . . .
> Lerneth to suffre, or elles, so moot I goon,
> Ye shul it lerne, wher so ye wole or noon;
> For in this world, certein, ther no wight is
> That he ne dooth or seith somtyme amys.
> Ire, siknesse, or constellacioun,
> Wyn, wo, or chaungynge of complexioun
> Causeth ful ofte to doon amys or speken. (v, 764–783)

Chaucer's two main points—that love dies if a couple keeps bickering about who is boss and that a successful marriage requires both patience and tolerance—are simple truths, commonplaces perhaps but much too well put to be banal.

It is not alone the good sense that irks many critics today but also the forthright way it is stated. They deplore anything overtly moral or didactic, preferring to believe that in Chaucer the fruit must be covered up with chaff (or that the fruit, when not thus covered up, is mere chaff). So in the Wife of Bath's Tale it is the chaff that gets critical approbation—the question raised and amusingly answered there about what it is that women really want and how the problem of who is to be boss can best be settled. The fruit—contained in the so-called pillow lecture, which is a long and serious discussion of the qualities one should want or hope for in a spouse—is shrugged off as an annoyance to be endured or an embarrassment to keep silent about.

The fourth and final basis for Chaucer's persuasiveness is that his views about love are clearly the product of thought, long and careful thought—the thought of a man who, despite all he had read about it or learned through his own experience, still found love perplexing. The fact that he admits this, repeatedly echoing the astonishment he had expressed early in his career at the "wonderful werkynge" of love and confessing that he couldn't really understand it at all, is not just a joke. And the fact that he does not profess to have found the final answers lends appeal as well as assurance to the answers he saw fit to venture.

To regard love in this way—thoughtfully, sensibly, and honestly—makes for a mode of treatment unlike the kind we have now come to expect. Instead of beguiling us with pretty sentiments, soaring fancies, and lofty ideals or dazzling us with exquisitely turned phrases, Chaucer gives us carefully wrought statements to cogitate. Chaucer's mode, a product of the mind rather than the emotions, lacks the lyricism of later English poets, who sing love's praises and its joys or sorrows with an intensity of feeling that he rarely displays. He strikes a true lyric note now and again—as for example in the song Troilus sings just after being suddenly smitten, beginning with the line "If no love is, O God, what fele I so?" (I, 400) or in the aubade of the two lovers, after their night together has come to an end, which Criseyde begins lamenting thus:

> "Myn hertes lif, my triste, and my plesaunce,
> That I was born, allas, what me is wo,
> That day of us moot make disseveraunce!"
> (III, 1422–1425)

Admirable as the note is, it is not sustained long enough nor sounded in such a way as to attract much notice. Indeed Chaucer seems to mute it quite deliberately, for instead of building up the lyric passages with suitable fanfare he plays them down, letting us enjoy them for what they are—delightful bits of decoration. Their omission would cause little serious damage to the poem and none whatever to the kind of love dealt with there.

In *Troilus* love is not merely displayed. It is probed. And it is the kind of love that bears up under Chaucer's probing, which is not only thoughtful, honest, and sensible but also sympathetic. To Chaucer's sympathetic concern we are expected to respond, and all of us do, except of course those who completely ignore his deeply expressed concern or choose to regard it as ironic.

If, as I have been trying to show, Chaucer has something interesting to say about love—interesting because it is still valid— he also manages to say it well. From a consideration of the substance of his love poetry, we therefore now turn to its technique, but instead of examining Chaucer's poetic technique in general, which quite obviously would carry us far afield, I shall call attention here to only two special features encountered exclusively in his treatment of love.

Love involves passion and passion involves its gratification. Where gratification is the sole consideration—that is, where it's not love at all but merely an itch—the problem posed is not very serious, for it is simply the question of how to handle fornication. Yet for a writer intent on achieving a permanent place in literature rather than a momentary and lucrative one, the problem is not trivial. It requires thought if for no other reason than to produce the effect which is desired. The effect Chaucer was after in his fabliaux was not to titillate his readers, or shock them, or disgust them but to set them laughing. This is why he handles fornication as he does there, treating it as a silly business and underscoring this by making it seem even sillier than in fact it usually is. To do so he relies on two time-tested devices. The one, which he employs in four of his best fabliaux, involves compounding the felony, so to speak, making it not simply fornication but fornication with someone else's wife, for cuckoldry has always seemed especially hilarious, in fiction at any rate. The other, which he also employs in three of these same fabliaux, is to have the fornication occur in a ludicrously impossible place—

in the branches of a pear tree, or in a bedroom with the husband present, or in separate tubs hung from the ceiling, although this last feat, to be sure, proved beyond Chaucer's imaginative powers.

The outcome of these shenanigans, we might note, involved no regrets, certainly not on the part of the most active participants—the women least of all, who not only enjoyed it all greatly but emerged completely unscathed, with hearts unbroken and without mischance offspring to commemorate the event. Nor were there regrets on the part of the pilgrims who heard these tales, not even the two nuns, who at the end of the Miller's Tale, the most rollicking of the lot, joined in the general laughter. If the reaction then was laughter rather than shocked silence or stern rebuke, it should come as no surprise to us. Indeed it ought to remind us that besides the Parson's uncompromising view of such goings-on, there were other views as well which even he could share on occasion and this time evidently did. Laughter is salutary, especially when, as is true of all Chaucer's fabliaux, there is an undercurrent of seriousness, enough at any rate to remind us, as these four tales do, that there is more to love than sex.

Love of the kind dealt with in *Troilus* also involves lovemaking, but it must of course be handled quite differently there. Occupying more than four hundred lines and constituting one of the finest passages of this sort in literature, it is treated with remarkable finesse. Almost completely devoid of any physical details and totally free of anything sordid, it succeeds nonetheless in being wholly erotic. This is as it should be, the love of Criseyde and Troilus requiring it and the poem demanding it. Imagine the result if the consummation scene were cut out in the poem!

Besides passion, however, their lovemaking involves tenderness—an exquisite tenderness expressible only by dwelling on it at some length. But this runs the risk of making it seem cloying—a calamitous effect which Chaucer avoided by the daring tack of introducing humor into the scene in the person of Pandarus. Whether Chaucer may not have overdone it, keeping Pandarus in the lovers' bedroom too long and letting him busy himself too much there solely for the effect it is meant to have upon us, since quite obviously it has none whatever on the lovers, is perhaps questionable. What is not questionable is that it works, the pungency of the humor cancelling out any excessive sweetness there and yet not depriving the scene of any of its necessary eroticism.

For the treatment of lovemaking, Chaucer might have followed the models at hand but, if he had, his fabliaux would have remained merely dirty jokes, good for a laugh and nothing more, and his *Troilus* a story concerned primarily with the carnal element in love.

For the other special feature meriting notice here, the treatment of love talk, there were no models at all. For though young couples had doubtlessly been whispering sweet nothings to each other for centuries, no writer had bothered with this before, presumably because it seemed too trivial for literary recognition. Chaucer was the first to give it the serious attention it needed, realizing that love talk is a special sort of language, differing from ordinary language in both form and content. It has its own distinctive style, its own vocabulary, and often even its own grammar and pronunciation. How closely he had observed it and how accurately he reproduced it is abundantly evident in *Troilus*. Of concern to us here are not all its odd little mannerisms, which I have dealt with elsewhere, but the one characteristic that sets love talk totally apart—the fact that its truth and falsity are not to be measured by what is said but by what is meant. And in love of the kind dealt with in *Troilus*, meaning is utterly equivocal, giving rise to lies that are not intended to delude anyone nor indeed should they. Both Criseyde and Troilus are aware that besides the purity of their love there is also its passion, and however delicately they conceal this, even from themselves, it is everpresent in their minds. Hence there is a curious ambivalence in their love talk, for truth and falsehood are inextricably mingled there and innocence and knowingness combined. And this is true of course not only of their talk but of the sweet nothings whispered by countless couples down through the ages.

The ambivalence of love talk makes it an art which, as any teenager can vouch, is readily grasped and which, as everyone has discovered, is easily misconstrued. It is also a delicate art to practice, particularly when the aim is not merely to give voice to it but to voice it effectively enough to exploit its literary possibilities. The first time this was successfully done was in *Troilus*. The wonder is not so much that it had never been tried before as that it has never since been done better.

Instead of appreciating this remarkable achievement, we are likely to pass over it lightly there, noting only how quaint or amusing the love talk seems in this poem written almost six hundred years ago. Or, forgetting that it is love talk, we may mistake its significance, seeking deeper meanings and motives than we should in the sweet nothings voiced there.

Chaucer himself warns us of this, pointing out, as we have already seen, that however *nyce* and *straunge* the love talk there may now seem, "thei spak hem so, and spedde as wel in love as men now do." About the error of taking such talk at face value, he is not quite so explicit and yet he is clear enough, repeatedly indicating that the lovers say both more and less than they really mean. And they do so quite consciously but without duplicity. Both were well-versed in the art, better versed apparently than many critics today, who seize upon some remark or other there as evidence of Troilus's insincerity or Criseyde's perfidy.

Their love talk, provided we recognize it for what it is, reveals better than anything else in the poem the nature of their love. If their "tender and passionate affection" for each other may be called ordinary love, then Chaucer, by probing it deeply and sympathetically and by giving it almost perfect expression, shows us how extraordinary such love indeed is. This is, I believe, what all love poets have sought to do. None have succeeded better than Chaucer.

Norman E. Eliason

Chaucer's Parodies of Love

In its customary use as a critical term, parody is taken to mean more or less the same thing as satire; and, using the term in this sense, Chaucerian critics have spoken of such works as the Miller's Tale as parodies of courtly love. As I am using the term, however, and as I suggest it may properly be used, parody is not at all the same as satire, or burlesque, or, for that matter, irony.[1] Still, we may understand parody by comparing it to satire.

Ordinarily in satire the given exists as a representative of something inadequate. The satiric process involves our awareness of this inadequacy and our going from the particular inadequacy to the general one, the "original," referred to by it. In parody, on the other hand, the process, as well as our response to it, is quite different. Although the given exists once again as something inadequate, we go from it and call up an ideal that exists, as it were, behind it. This ideal is not contained or fully reflected in the given, as in satire. Rather, when we call up the ideal, we are aware of the gap between it and the given. We see just how inadequate the given is, and in this awareness lies the creation of humor. But parody does not, like satire, just make fun of the given: it insists that we see it in terms of something that is adequate. In having us call up this corrective, this ideal, the given necessarily brings into being an additional frame of reference.

To illustrate simply what I mean, we may look at the portrait of the Friar in the General Prologue to the *Canterbury Tales*. This portrait, for all its mockery, does something more than satirize friars. In seeing the inadequacies of Friar Huberd, we necessarily

1. As a critical term, parody (from Greek *parōdia*) came into classical Latin rhetorical theory and criticism as "a name drawn from songs sung in imitation of others, but employed by an abuse of language to designate imitation in verse or prose" (Quintilian, *Institutio Oratoria*, ix.ii.35, Loeb Classical Library, iii, 395). The term came into English critical usage in the late eighteenth century. In modern criticism, Northrop Frye, for example, uses the term as a theme, as "the mocking of the exuberant play of art by suggesting its imitation in terms of 'real life' " (*Anatomy of Criticism: Four Essays*, Princeton: Princeton University Press, 1957, p. 147). I use the term to refer less to the imitation than to the process of calling up the "original."

call up the ideal of friars, the original concept and work of Saint Francis and Saint Dominic, for instance. This is the frame of reference behind Huberd, that which is reflected so imperfectly in him. We are thus aware of not just the inadequacies but the ideal as well.

In like manner, to take an example from the secular pilgrims, the portrait of the Wife of Bath represents not so much a satire on women or wives as a parody of the ideal of woman, which for the Christian Middle Ages was represented by the Virgin Mary. It is in terms of this parody that we may best understand the significance of the details of weaving and of clothing in general in the Wife's description. The Virgin was famous for weaving the cloth without a seam, an allegorical way of referring—with seamless equalling sinless—to her giving birth to Christ.[2] But the Wife of Bath is defined in terms of the business of cloth-making and of the vestments of this world; and, significantly, she is barren, without offspring. Just as Mary is called the Virgin, so Alisoun of Bath is ironically called the Wife. The love that the Wife reveals and revels in is quite different from that associated with Mary, and continuing the irony, the Wife is frequently "out of alle charitee" (I, 452),[3] especially with those who go to the offering before her. The Wife's "offering," of self-centered earthly passion, is a parody of the celestial love "offered" by Mary and by those who are selflessly concerned with Christian charity.

We should not think that the ideal is lessened or in any way cheapened by its being parodied. Parody is in fact possible because the ideal is precisely that. It provides a level or background of truth that is always present and constant. No matter what goes on in the foreground, the background truth is no whit the less. So in medieval nativity plays we can have the parody of Christ's birth in the scene in the *Second Shepherd's Play* where Mak and his wife put a sheep in a cradle. Similarly, in the plays that show the midwives doubting Mary's virginity, the sanctity of the Virgin is untouched. As

2. The Virgin as a weaver of such garb is a commonplace in the Marian hymns. She is also described as the "weaver" of Christ's fleshly garb: see Chaucer's Second Nun's Prologue (VIII, 42).

3. All quotations from Chaucer are according to *The Works of Geoffrey Chaucer*, ed. F. N. Robinson, 2nd ed. (Boston: Houghton Mifflin, 1957).

the Middle Ages well knew, sobriety is not the handmaiden or spokesman of Truth; and, conversely, seriousness and humor may well go hand in hand.

There is, of course, much satire in Chaucer. But along with this satire—perhaps even more important than it—is parody, which I would say is Chaucer's predominant way of looking at this world. In each instance when we are aware of an ideal behind a given, this ideal is a major Christian concept or value. The Man of Law, for example, makes us aware of that archetypal man of law, Christ, as well as the new law, including the concept of justice brought to the world with him. In seeing the inadequacies of Chaucer's pilgrim Man of Law—who seems to be one thing while we know he is actually another—we become aware of an ideal justice not compromised or flawed. Perhaps we may thus come to understand something of the Virtue of Justice, which should be one of the characteristics of the Christian in this world and one of the cornerstones of Christian society.

Even Chaucer's narrative device of the pilgrimage makes use of parody. The journey from the Tabard Inn encompassed by Miller and Reeve, and guided by tavernkeeper Harry Bailly— himself a parody of the Christian concept of Host, man's proper spiritual food—summons up the ideal pilgrimage to God that every Christian is called upon to make. But there is no spiritual progress in the journey made by Chaucer's "ordinary" men and women. Instead of spiritually ascending during their three-day journey, they by and large stay wholly on earthly roads eating earthly food and thinking earthly thoughts. From their beginning at the Tabard Inn, described as being "faste by the Belle" (I, 719), apparently a notorious brothel, they stay in the figurative Babylons of this world. The best that most of them can do may be represented symbolically by the little town they pass by called "Bobbe-up-and-doun." And this town is said to be "under the Blee," perhaps a play on *bleyne*, meaning "to blemish" (IX, 2–3).

Without going into the matter in further detail here we may say that parody functions in the *Canterbury Tales* to call up another level of reality, that of the Christian ideal, which gives point and purpose to the surface level. It acts as our basis for understanding the given. Through parody we thus know what is and what ideally should be. Such a view as this is in accord with the medieval Augustinian view of this world as not just an inadequate representation of the more real otherworld but as the main way for man to know the otherworld. Through the book of nature—resembling the inadequate *littera*, or surface, of a literary work—man may glimpse intimations of a greater reality. Indeed, if he fails to do this, he then fails to recognize and use the aids God has put at his disposal for understanding Him and for attaining the otherworld. Man may recognize that this world is insignificant, even ridiculous; but it is more important for him to sense the sufficiency of what is beyond it.

Now back to Chaucer and love. Necessarily, and not unexpectedly, the medieval ideal of love—that known to man through his understanding of Christ's incarnation and through his awareness of the concept of charity in Christian teaching—is not often stated explicitly in Chaucer's narrative writings. But a lack of overt didacticism does not mean that these poems are void of *significatio*, or what Chaucer would call *sentence*. The profusion of surface *mirthe* in Chaucer should not make us assume that there is consequently no *doctryne*, no meaning or teaching that gives point to the *mirthe*. And sometimes the *doctryne* of Christian love is clearly stated. The best, or at least the most noteworthy, statement of this ideal appears in the so-called epilogue to *Troilus and Criseyde*. There, after showing us the inadequate, ultimately unsatisfying love that has as its object something transitory and mutable, Chaucer calls our attention to love of God:

> O yonge, fresshe folkes, he or she,
> In which that love up groweth with youre age,
> Repeyreth hom fro worldly vanyte,
> And of youre herte up casteth the visage
> To thilke God that after his ymage
> Yow made, and thynketh al nys but a faire
> This world, that passeth soone as floures faire.
> And loveth hym, the which that right for love
> Upon a crois, oure soules for to beye,
> First starf, and roos, and sit in hevene above;
> For he nyl falsen no wight, dar I seye,
> That wol his herte al holly on hym leye.
> And syn he best to love is, and most meke,
> What nedeth feynede loves for to seke? (v, 1835–1848)

This is both the ideal and the corrective to inadequate frustrating love. It may be regarded as the amorous equivalent to the Parson's words at the end of the *Canterbury Tales* about "the endelees blisse of hevene" that is the fruit of penance and that lies at the end of man's proper journey through life (x, 1076). In each instance, in both *Troilus and Criseyde* and the *Canterbury Tales*, the explicit statement of the ideal comes as a corrective, after we have witnessed and presumably come to realize the inadequacies of that love that looks to and remains in this world.

Most of the time, however, Chaucer creates a narrative surface that parodies this ideal love. Its rich details, far from being realistic *per se*, exist to create a response to the worldly that emphasizes the need for something more adequate. In his early writings Chaucer uses the ideal of love in some interesting and typical ways—even in the *Book of the Duchess*, his earliest long poem, though we might at first wonder whether the ideal appears here at all. It certainly is not to be found in the dead lady, even though she is idealized by the man in black; she is not an ideal since she and the knight's love lead only to death. She has died, and her lover, melancholic and full of despair, seems to be on the verge of death. Nor is the ideal to be found in the forlorn narrator who opens the poem. This *mased* creature, full of *fantasies*, does not know "what is best to doo" (29). He does not even know how to get sleep, much less love; yet even he knows that there is no "phisicien but oon" that can heal him of his eight-year sickness (36–40).

Nor is the ideal of love to be found in the tragic story of Seys and Alcione that the narrator finds in the romance he takes to "drive the night away" (49). This story ends with Alcione's learning of the death of her husband Seys, but instead of heeding his advice to "Awake! let be your sorwful lyf! / For in your sorwe there lyth no red" (202–203), she continues to lament and dies on "the thridde morwe" (214). Such a detail as dying on the third morning is a parodic one in that it may function to call up the corrective and counter-image of Christ's rising from death on the third day. Unlike this resurrection, there is in the case of Alcione only sorrow and additional death. Her love for her husband leads not to a proper understanding of mutability or of the transitoriness of earthly things, but rather to her own despair and subsequent destruction. As a figure of improper love, as one unable to understand dreams, and as one who cannot "awake," she acts as a mirror-image of the narrator—who also seems to be death-seeking, if that is what his excessive desire for sleep signifies. And, again ironically, this narrator sees in the story of Seys and Alcione a way to obtain sleep. Such is hardly the proper *doctryne* to be taken from the tale. His ridiculous action of bribing Juno with a mattress shows that he has clearly misunderstood its *sentence*. More humorously, the bribe seems to work, for he gets the sleep he has been after—we might be tempted to say "the sleep he has been dying for."

Having seen that this narrator is unable to understand the meaning of things, that he misinterprets the *littera*, we can hardly trust him to be a guide. If he is responsible for making the man in black finally comprehend and accept the death of his lady, the point is very ironic. He and the man in black—a figure of death, who, despairing, sits with his back to "an ook, an huge tree" (445)—are truly brothers. The setting is suggestive of a place of death—we may compare the description of death found under the oak tree in the Pardoner's Tale (VI, 765). Without his realizing it, the narrator has met in this setting a figure of sorrow such as he himself is. The complaint he hears from the black knight contains "the moste pitee, the moste rowthe" (465) he has ever heard; but there is no virtue in grief, as every authority from at least Solomon to Chaucer's own *Tale of Melibee* maintains: it is a brother to death and even leads to it. In his mourning and lamenting, the black knight shows as little comprehension of proper love and of the proper use of worldly things as the narrator or Alcione. Then, we might wonder, where is the corrective to this inadequate destructive love? Where indeed lies that which functions as the opposite of the death-bringing sorrow so much in evidence in the *littera* of this poem? The answer is found in the first scene of the narrator's dream, that which is between his reading of Seys and Alcione and his dialogue with the man in black.

The details are significant. The narrator awakens in the May dawn: he is in his bed "al naked" (293), and the sound of birds is all around him, "Was never herd so swete a steven, / But hyt had be a thyng of heven" (307–308). On the windows of his chamber is painted "al the story of Troye," and on the walls appear "bothe text and glose, / Of al the Romaunce of the Rose" (333–334). These references have clear connections with love; but Troy was a type of the destructive way of earthly love, and the *Roman de la Rose* was far more than a tale of the attainment of earthly love. Primarily, at least in Jean de Meun's rendition, it was an indictment of such love and an exhortation, as Reason's words make clear, for men to follow another and better love. Significantly, it appears here with "bothe text and glose," the narrative and its exegesis.

As the dreamer lies in bed, he hears a hunting horn, and, going outside, he meets the hunters. Speaking to one of them, he asks,

> "Say, felowe, who shal hunte here?"
> Quod I, and he answered ageyn,
> "Syr, th'emperour Octovyen,"
> Quod he, "and ys here faste by."
> "A Goddes half, in good tyme!" quod I,
> "Go we faste!" and gan to ryde. (366–371)

And with these words the dreamer joins Octavian's hunt. When the *forloyn* is blown, indicating that the hart has escaped the hunters, the dreamer walks "fro my tree," where apparently he had stationed himself. A fawning dog nuzzles him and leads him "Doun by a floury grene wente / Ful thikke of gras, ful softe and swete" (398–399), to a grove of great trees, where he sees the man in black sitting under an oak.

The specific context enabling us to understand the ensuing dialogue and to see in perspective the inadequate destructive loves that fill this poem is contained in this hunt scene. Whereas the allegory of the hart hunt, as well as the hart-heart paronomasia, has long been recognized, the role of Octavian here has not been much discussed. While this figure may function in terms of topical allegory as a portrayal of Edward iii or John of Gaunt,[4] the reference is most immediately to the Roman emperor Octavian, also known as Caesar Augustus. During the Middle Ages this ancient ruler was primarily identified as the monarch at the time of the birth of Christ and, moreover, as the earthly counterpart of Christ. Supported by the famous "render unto Caesar"

4. See the discussion in Robinson, p. 775, n. 368. See also Joseph E. Grennen, "*Hert-huntyng* in the *Book of the Duchess*," *MLQ*, xxv (1964), 131–139; and Mother Angela Carson, "The Sovereignty of Octovyen in the *Book of the Duchess*," *AnM*, viii (1967), 41–58.

lesson, the idea was reinforced by the *Pax Augusta* and by the fact that Christ chose to come to mankind at the time when the perfect emperor was there, ruling the world in a state of perfect peace. As Dante, for example, maintained, "the world had been at its best when mankind was guided by Divus Augustus . . . under whose reign Christ himself chose to become man, and for that matter, a Roman citizen."[5]

The proof positive for the Middle Ages lay in the well-known story of Octavian's hearing of the birth of Christ from the Tibertine sibyl, and accepting the child as his lord. As a typical scene in the medieval drama indicates, Octavian was frequently viewed as a first convert to Christ and as the monarch whose rule heralded and led to that of Christ. In the Chester cycle, for instance, Octavian not only states that Christ is most worthy and that he will be his subject, but tells his people to forego worshiping him and turn to Christ.[6] As medieval typological exegetes viewed the legend, Octavian was a *figura* of Christ, and the very existence of this temporal ruler suggested the imminence of the heavenly ruler. Also, to go from Octavian to Christ was regarded as going from earthly to the heavenly. As Otto of Freising wrote in the twelfth century, "the reign of Augustus was in many ways a prophecy of the reign of Christ"; and as one of the Worcester Sermons states, "Be this Octouian ich vndirstonde a tis tyme owr Kyng & owr Emperour, Crist, Godes sone of heuene."[7]

The presence of Octavian may thus be seen to indicate the imminent coming of Christ. When the dreamer in the *Book of the Duchess* hears that it is the emperor Octavian who is hunting, he responds with enthusiasm: "A Goddes half, in good tyme," that is, literally translated "On God's behalf" (or "In God's name"); "it's about time." Time, we might wonder, for what? The answer is, time for the Second Coming of Christ. The horns of the hunt are in this sense those announcing Judgment Day.

Inherent in the *Book of the Duchess* from beginning to end is the idea of death and rebirth. The dreamer at the beginning is "a

5. *Monarchia*, I.16. Cf. *Purgatorio*, XXXII, 102.
6. "The Nativity," 11.685–688, in *The Chester Plays*, ed. Hermann Deimling, Early English Text Society, Extra Series 62 (London, 1892), I, 13.
7. Otto, *De duabus civitatibus*, III.6, trans. C. C. Mierow, *The Two Cities* (New York: Columbia University Press, 1928); Worcester Sermon, in *Three Middle English Sermons from the Worcester Chapter MS. F.10*, ed. D. M. Grisdale (Kendal: University of Leeds, 1939).

mased thyng" (12), a walking dead man, and, indeed, lack of sleep and general despair have slain his spirit "of quyknesse," of life (26). His suffering has been for eight years, a number that may have symbolic value in this poem. Chaucer may, in fact, be indicating to us how we should view such numbers when he refers to "Argus, the noble counter," that is, to Al-Kwārizm, a significant Arab mathematician, who says that men may know all things through numbers (435–440). Through number, according to authorities from the Book of Wisdom (11:20) and the Church Fathers, man may comprehend the essential reality and full meaning of God's creation.

In terms of medieval number symbolism, eight is the traditional number of rebirth and resurrection. Since creation took place in seven days, the eighth day was seen as representing a renewal, a new beginning.[8] The sleep the Chaucerian dreamer wishes for so much exists, as we have seen, as a symbolic death. In terms of this, his awakening—"in my bed al naked"—at dawn in the springtime of the world is a type of rebirth. The presence of Octavian, whose name also contains the symbolic concept of eight, memorializes, as it were, the imminent rebirth. But, more important to the ostensible subject of the poem, love, the scene brings to the work a kind of love that has not appeared so far, one that functions as the opposite of and as the corrective to the debilitating, death-bringing love seen over and over.

Octavian's hart hunt makes use of a commonplace from medieval Celtic lore and Christian symbolism. Such a hunt may refer symbolically to the hunt of the devil for the souls of sinners, in the hound-of-hell motif; but it may also refer to the hunt of Christ to save man. Presumably the hunt in the *Book of the Duchess* forms the background to the dialogue between the narrator and the man in black. That is, it goes on while the two men talk— functioning in this sense as Bercilak's hunts in *Sir Gawain and the Green Knight* do in forming a background for the conversation between Gawain and Bercilak's wife, again a conversation about love. With the final assertion of the death of the black knight's lady, we return to the hunt: "And with that word ryght anoon / They gan to strake forth; al was doon, / For that tyme, the

8. On eight, see, e.g., Bede, *De templo Salomonis*, ii.25 (*PL*, 91: 806); and Rabanus Maurus, *De universo*, xviii.3 (*PL*, 111: 491).

hert-huntyng" (1311–1313). At this point it appears to the narrator that "this kyng" (1314) rides home to "A long castel with walles white, / Be seynt Johan! on a ryche hil" (1318–1319). Although "this kyng" is often taken to be the man in black, he is but a knight and is never referred to as a king. Rather, the king seems to be Octavian again; and the long castle on the rich hill he rides to is, notwithstanding the possible play on Lancaster and Richmond, the heavenly Jerusalem. The exclamation, "Be seynt Johan!" as a reference to the Book of Revelations, clearly reinforces this sense.

Something is obviously finished, and a catharsis or release of sorts appears to have taken place. The final sound in the dream is of a bell tolling twelve times (1322–1323). The day is over; it is time for time to begin again. Also, with this universal number twelve, representing the combination of the physical number four and the spiritual number three, the narrator awakens, this time back in the world of worldly reality, and the poem ends. The main point is not whether the narrator has understood his dream but whether we the audience are able to comprehend the kinds of love presented to us and to see that the conflict inherent in the narrator from the beginning is a false one, occurring because of his inadequate understanding of love and his improper view of earthly objects.

A version of heavenly love seems to be explicitly presented in the *Parliament of Fowls* when, in the Macrobius account of the dream of Scipio, the narrator hears that those who "lovede commune profyt" should obtain "a blysful place. . . . There as joye is that last withouten ende" (47–49). What is emphasized here, however, is the other side of the contemplative coin—not the love of heavenly things but the contempt for earthly things. Because of this reversal Chaucer is able to use this *contemptus mundi* view in direct contrast to that of his narrator, who is so *astoned* by love that "Nat wot I wel wher that I flete or synke" (7). As I have argued elsewhere, instead of representing a solution to the narrator's problems of love, this *contemptus* view makes him "fulfyld of thought and busy hevynesse"; for, as he goes on to say, "bothe I hadde thyng which that I nolde, / And ek I nadde that thyng that I wolde" (89–91).[9] The dream of Scipio is then

9. Edmund Reiss, "Troilus and the Failure of Understanding," *MLQ*, xxix

parodied in the narrator's own version of Scipio's experience, as the love of the common good recommended to Scipio (74–75) is parodied in the debate of the birds about love. In this debate both courtly fowls of *ravyne* and bourgeois water fowls reveal a selfish love that is hardly noble and that is far from resembling charity.

That the *contemptus mundi* attitude was only one side—and not the most important one—of the coin may be demonstrated by the plan of that apparent champion of the *contemptus* position, Pope Innocent III, to write a work on the worth of creation, paralleling his famous treatise on the scorn of worldly things. This work, emphasizing the dignity of man, would doubtless have been well within the Augustinian tradition emphasizing the essential goodness of God's creation. It would have represented a positive approach to the subject of how to view this world.[10]

In the *Parliament of Fowls* we may have Chaucer's first real attempt to suggest that love in the world governed by Nature is not a priori at odds with love of God. His proposal seems to be that we must regard a juxtaposition of the two loves as a false dichotomy, and achieve a synthesis between the two views that will mirror the hierarchical order of this world and the other world. But, while this poem continues and goes beyond what is brought up in the *Book of the Duchess*, it still does not fully solve the problem. This solution is, as we have seen, best presented at the end of the *Troilus and Criseyde*, which is Chaucer's most explicit recommendation about how man should live and love.

Love also provides the dominant subject and the most pervasive theme of the *Canterbury Tales*. And again Chaucer's method is primarily one of parody. Without running through the complete *Tales* to demonstrate this, we may look at a single group of tales, those, say, that make up Fragment I, the first day of pilgrimage, those of the Knight, Miller, Reeve, and Cook.

In the Knight's Tale divine love is most obviously parodied in Palamon's initial response to Emelye. Viewing her as a goddess, he falls onto his knees and prays to her (I, 1101 ff.). Arcite's

---

(1968), esp. 131–137.

10. The plan is stated in the Prologue to his *De miseria humanae conditionis*. Cf. Augustine, e.g., *Confessionum*, VII.xii.18 (*PL*, 32:743); *De doctrina Christiana*, I. xxiv.24 (*PL*, 34: 28); *De vera religione*, XVIII.35–36 (*PL*, 34:137); *Enchiridion*, XIII.4 (*PL*, 40: 238); also, in the late Middle Ages, Thomas Aquinas, *Summa Theologiae*, I.65.2; II–II.25.5.

response is no better, for he asserts that unless he has "hir mercy and hir grace . . . I nam but deed" (1120 ff.). Here in these typical postures of courtly love is the essence of the courtly parody of divine love, where both the mechanics and the terminology of the love are taken as being equal to the convert's fervent need for God. That the language and fervency of the seducer and the imminent martyr resemble each other is clearly intentional, and humor is very much a result of this resemblance. The posture of the typical courtly lover is, as medievalists are beginning to realize, one of ludicrous excess.[11] Although we today might take such sentimentality seriously, we should not deceive ourselves into thinking that the Middle Ages could seriously equate lust with religious emotion. Alongside the desires of the soul, those of the body are necessarily trivial. The situation of the body's presenting itself as important as the soul is like that of the jester's pretending to be king.

And even within the realm of earthly love it is necessary to distinguish levels of emotion. Troilus in Book I, seeing Criseyde for the first time and falling in love with her, is a creature of folly as he takes to his bed and weeps and wails. We do not take his plight seriously, and we correctly laugh at him. But in a parallel scene in Book IV, when Troilus hears that Criseyde will be traded to the Greeks, and again retreats to his chamber for more moaning and groaning, we feel that his grief is real and he no longer seems so ridiculous to us. Still, the traits he exhibits at this time are those he showed in Book I. It is ironic that he can make no qualitative distinction between the two feelings, but such is the excess of the desire manifesting itself as courtly love. It and its concomitant frustration are all-embracing and all-consuming, possessing neither moderation nor perspective. It is furthermore ironic that the "new love" of Palamon and Arcite should destroy their own love, their friendship—which is a form of right or good loving—so that these blood brothers seek to kill each other.

The destructive power of earthly desire is seen even more clearly in the Knight's Tale in the Temple of Venus which Theseus causes to be constructed for the fight between Palamon and

11. See, e.g., D. W. Robertson, Jr., *A Preface to Chaucer: Studies in Medieval Perspectives* (Princeton: Princeton University Press, 1962), pp. 391 ff.; and several of the essays in *The Meaning of Courtly Love,* ed. F. X. Newman (Albany: State University of New York Press, 1968).

Arcite. The various carvings and portraits within this temple are

> ful pitous to biholde,
> The broken slepes, and the sikes colde,
> The sacred teeris, and the waymentynge,
> The firy strokes of the desirynge
> That loves servantz in this lyf enduren. (1919–1923)

The temple is full of images of those who have been caught up by love "Til they for wo ful ofte seyde 'allas' " (1952).

This Temple of Venus is little different from that of Mars, showing those who have been destroyed by war and violence, and that of Diana, portraying the destructive power of prideful chastity. Like all earthly desires and goods rendered excessive, love is necessarily destructive. Chaucer's picture of it in the Knight's Tale amply illustrates the medieval commonplace that worldly desire leads man to death. Only when such love is put in a proper perspective and made servant to nobler feelings can it be redeemed and man escape from its power. When it results in marriage, with its emphasis on propagation—when, in other words, it has as its end regeneration rather than sensual satisfaction—it is rendered innocuous and can actually function as a means to human happiness.

Such the Knight's Tale shows us, but not unambiguously, for there are all sorts of qualifications about Theseus' purposes and his solution of marrying Palamon and Emelye, even though he quotes Boethius.[12] And there are similar ramifications of which the Knight is apparently unaware as he presents Theseus' solution to us as an ideal. The Knight's position that this marriage will make "of sorwes two / O parfit joye, lastynge everemo" (3071–3072), as well as his contention that Palamon now exists "in alle wele, / Lyvynge in blisse, in richesse, and in heele" (3101–3102), is a dubious one, even though it is in accord with the Knight's optimistic or comic view of creation as is seen in the words he uses to interrupt the Monk's Tale of *tragedie* and assert the opposite of the sad ending:

> And the contrarie is joye and greet solas,

12. His solution seems primarily dictated by political expediency, e.g., I, 2970 ff.

As whan a man hath been in povre estaat,
And clymbeth up and wexeth fortunat,
And there abideth in prosperitee.
Swich thyng is gladsom, as it thynketh me,
And of swich thyng were goodly for to telle. (vii, 3964–
3969)

And such a thing was what the Knight spoke of in his tale: this "waxing fortunate" is precisely what happened to Palamon, and in the Knight's view he finally "abideth in prosperitee." But it is doubtful, according to the medieval view of existence, whether one can find abiding prosperity in this world. And it is even more doubtful whether such prosperity can be the result of earthly love—even that ending in marriage.

The Knight's solution—like, I might add, the virtues seen in the man—is finally dubious and illusory.[13] In his solution we have what is not the final answer to the question of how one can and should love, but a first answer. Although Theseus' arrangement may appear to be a final solution, marriage presents far more problems than the naively optimistic Knight apparently realizes. The question of sovereignty in marriage, for instance, does not come up yet; but when it does, we easily see the breakdown of the Knight's facile solution.

The inadequacy of the Knight's answer is what allows his tale to be burlesqued in the ensuing Miller's Tale. This fabliau is doing all sorts of things, but its avowed purpose is to pay back the Knight. As the drunken Miller asserts,

By armes, and by blood and bones,
I kan a noble tale for the nones,
With which I wol now quite the Knyghtes tale. (3125–
3127)

The juxtaposition of such blasphemy and the term "noble" sets the tone for what follows in this barnyard version of courtly love. The depiction begins with the description of the learned clerk *hende* Nicholas, who is adept at such love: "Of deerne love he

13. The "chivalrie, / Trouthe and honour, fredom and curtesie" professed by the Knight (i, 45–46), are controverted by such deeds as his fighting as a mercenary for a heathen lord (i, 64 ff.).

koude and of solas" (3200). But Nicholas goes the gentle Knight
of the previous tale one better in that *solas* is very important to
him. Thus, as he speaks to Alisoun of his *deerne love* for her, he
"caughte hire by the queynte" and "heeld hire harde by the
haunchebones" (3276 ff.). The juxtaposition of word and deed
functions to satirize the language of the courtly lover; and, when
Alisoun responds with "Do wey youre handes, for youre curteis-
ye" (3287), we realize further how far such courtesy is from the
Christian ideal.

Along with this burlesque, however, there is also parody, in the
sense that we have been using the term. The Miller's statement
that he will tell "a legende and a lyf / Bothe of a carpenter and
of his wyf" (3141–3142) calls up several possible reference points,
but notably the biblical story of Joseph and Mary. This suggestion is reinforced when we hear of Nicholas's singing the *"Ange-
lus ad virginem"* (3216), and in part when we hear Absolon's
parody of the Song of Songs as he woos Alisoun. Parody in fact
permeates the Miller's Tale: Nicholas's misuse of the story of
Noah's Flood is the most obvious example; but more important
than the biblical episodes, images, and lines that are called up is
the meaning behind them—what, that is, these references represented to Chaucer's audience. The child of Joseph and Mary
represented Love personified coming to the world of ordinary
men; the Song of Songs was viewed as a symbolic statement of
perfect divine love and of the mystical relationship between
Christ and the Church; and even the story of the Flood was taken
as representing finally an account of God's love for man—divine
justice gives way to divine love as God decides not to destroy his
creation. But in the Miller's Tale the holy love, mystical love, and
cosmic love suggested by these biblical references disappear, or
rather are subsumed under earthly desire. This, illicit and self-
centered, is all that appears in the narrative of the tale. That
Nicholas and Absolon are members of the clergy adds to the
irony of the piece. Each lover perverts the Christian idea of love,
and instead of expressing charity, each is concerned only with his
own good.

The Knight's Tale presented love as a noble sentiment—misdi-
rected and destructive, but still ostensibly noble; the Miller's Tale
shows it as a passion, as unadulterated adultery—perhaps what
the noble love of the Knight's Tale in fact is. There is a progres-

sion of sorts here, for the first group of tales in the *Canterbury Tales* presents a constant and distinct lowering or reduction of love. In the Reeve's Tale, love is seen as the result not of passion but of revenge. Neither Clerk, John or Aleyn, desires the Miller's wife or daughter for herself. As Aleyn says to his fellow,

> If that I may, yon wenche wil I swyve.
> Som esement has lawe yshapen us;
> For, John, ther is a lawe that says thus,
> That gif a man in a point be agreved,
> That in another he sal be releved. (4178–4182)

Not only is Aleyn defendant, he is also jury and judge. He assesses his loss, finds the Miller guilty, and fixes the retribution. Such justice is clearly a perversion of the real thing; but, more important, Aleyn's eye-for-an-eye, tooth-for-a-tooth concept of justice calls up the Old Law, and denies the New Law of Christianity, where love, not justice, is the ideal. In the Reeve's Tale love is used as a means of justice but in a way that perverts the Christian view.

Likewise, when John, lying alone in bed, muses about his situation, he rationalizes that Aleyn has "somwhat for his harm" (4203). He too desires redress, and in order to avoid being held "a daf, a cokenay," when that story "is tald another day" (4207–4208), he moves the cradle and tricks the Miller's wife into his bed. Here is not only a substitution of lechery for true love or even for wedded bliss; it is also a flagrant violation of the fruits of marriage—the children—which are here being used as the vehicles for illicit love. But can Aleyn's and John's feelings really be called love? Hardly. When Aleyn says to the Miller's daughter, "Fare weel, Malyne, sweete wight! . . . I is thyn awen clerk, swa have I seel" (4236–4239), his words are not only a burlesque of the literary *aube;* they also represent a parody of what should be a true clerk's affirmation. Instead of Malyne (Molly), his lady should be the Virgin Mary—whose very name is echoed in Malyne's. Not only does Aleyn not serve the Virgin, he is instrumental in making sure that his lady is not a virgin. The tale thus represents the violation—under the pretext of justice—of the sanctity of matrimony and chastity, and results in a perverse, warped set of values that, ironically, creates the happy ending of the piece.

The lowering of love surely would have continued in detail in the

Cook's Tale. But, incomplete as the tale is, we can still see that it was
to be about love. The main character, Perkyn Revelour, was "as
ful of love and paramour / As is the hyve ful of hony sweete"
(4372–4373). Another main character is the wife who "swyved for
hir sustenance" (4422). Here love seems to be mainly a business.
In the Reeve's Tale love had been expressed in terms of revenge,
but revenge was still a human feeling. In the Cook's Tale love is
depersonalized: it becomes something to barter with, the equivalent of money; and, as one of the goods of this world, it is far from
its ideal celestial form.

While Chaucer's writings are filled with instances showing the
gap between the ideal and the given, his work is permeated by the
attempt to reconcile the spiritual ideals of Christian love with the
physical feelings and desires of mortal human love. If anything,
this attempt represents the dominant theme of his poetry and his
main overall way of using love. The unsatisfied, frustrated lover
is a ludicrous figure, but at the same time, as the *Troilus* demonstrates, he is the basis of tragedy. Laughing at the lover is necessary as a corrective to taking him seriously and possibly enno-
bling his perverse feelings. But such laughter is hardly sufficient.
It is likewise not enough to say to this lover, stop loving an earthly
love and turn your thoughts to the heavens. This has always been
more easily said than done. The role of the lover is a difficult one
to assess, to use properly, and, for that matter, to escape. Few
men would choose to follow Origen's example of self-castration,
and even Origen was criticized for his fervent asceticism. The
view of total removal from the world was always regarded by
orthodox Christians as an excessive one, and from the time of the
Valentinians and Donatists to and beyond that of the Cathars,
the Christian's isolation from the world around him was properly
considered to be eschatological rather than sociological.

The problem then is a psychological one, and Chaucer must
have known well such arguments as those used by Reason against
worldly love and about the destructive power of passion in Jean
de Meun's *Roman de la Rose* (4199–4328).[14] He could also see
here the concomitant problems of the Lover in reconciling these
arguments with his strong desires. The "perfect love" that Reason
counsels is, as the Lover realizes, not to be found upon the earth

14. Jean de Meun, *Le Roman de la Rose*, ed. Felix Lecoy (Paris, 1965).

(5388–5392). But this does not mean that such love does not exist. One may approximate it by loving the common good (5405–5428) and by realizing that charity is "a greater necessity than justice" (5444–5666).

Man is called upon not to remove himself from this world but, rather, to free himself from servitude to it, and, as he leads the active life, to use the world as his way to God. To learn the proper nature and use of love is, to be sure, a difficult task. As a first step, so Chaucer insists throughout his earlier dream narratives as well as in his later writings, one must recognize that earthly love does not have to be the opposite of heavenly love. Rather than be juxtaposed, the two states properly exist in a hierarchical order, with earthly love ultimately being the way to heavenly love. As the days in the week lead to the Sabbath, so should worldly love lead man to that which is celestial, and in neither case does the end result in a denial or a denigration of the means.

Although Chaucer investigates the problems of love over and over and suggests the answer to man's difficulties, his characters rarely show the awareness he asks from us, his audience. The *Melibee* is important as a definitive statement of the working of Christian charity, and the Second Nun's Tale is fundamental as a dramatic statement of the ideal marriage. But the plight of the ordinary lover—the stuff of Chaucer's narratives—will remain until he chooses to master his love rather than let it master him, until, that is, he attains Chaucer's perspective and can look at the given from the position of the ideal behind it.

Edmund Reiss

Chaucer's Marriage Group*

When I was asked to read a paper at the University of North Carolina a couple of years ago, I told the program chairman that I had what I fondly thought of as a polished paper on a vexed passage in Dante's *Commedia*, complete with slides, canned jokes, and the other apparatus of learned discourse; or that I could conflate my five weeks of course lectures on the "Marriage Group" into the semblance of a unified paper, trusting the audience to be tolerant of whatever incoherence that might involve. After some meditation we decided on the second plan; and it was a sobering experience to discover that my five weeks of lecture notes, once their irrelevancies had been deleted, did in fact manage to fill just about forty-five minutes. It is this same paper that I plan to inflict on you this morning, and with the same reservations.

Everyone knows about Kittredge's proposal that the *Canterbury Tales* includes a group of stories dealing specifically with the subject of marriage.[1] As usually defined, this "Marriage Group" consists of the Wife of Bath's Prologue and the Wife of Bath's Tale; then (after an interlude formed by the Friar's Tale and Summoner's Tale), the Clerk's Tale and the Merchant's Tale; and finally (after another interlude formed by the Squire's Tale), the Franklin's Tale. We may also notice incidentally an idea first proposed by W. W. Lawrence[2] —that there is a kind of introduction to this group, formed by the Tale of Melibee and the Nun's Priest's Tale. The Nun's Priest's Tale, with its lack of reverence for female wisdom and its gay piling-up of authorities, would then lead directly to the Wife of Bath's beginning outburst:

---

* This paper has been presented at a number of universities, including the University of North Carolina, the University of Toronto, Harvard University, Yale University, and Stanford University.

1. G. L. Kittredge, "Chaucer's Discussion of Marriage," *MP*, ix (1912), 435–467.

2. "The Marriage Group in the *Canterbury Tales*," *MP*, xi (1913), 247–258; and *Chaucer and the Canterbury Tales* (New York: Columbia University Press, 1950), pp. 119–144.

> Experience, though noon auctoritee
> Were in this world, is right ynogh for me
> To speke of wo that is in mariage. (III, 1–3)[3]

Now Kittredge's proposal of a "Marriage Group," extending with some interruptions from the Wife of Bath's Prologue to the Franklin's Tale, has of course met with a good bit of skepticism— usually centered in the basic objection that since the great majority of the *Canterbury Tales* deal in some way with sex or marriage, there is no reason for singling out this group of tales as dealing with it in a particular way. If we do assume the existence of a "Marriage Group" including this prologue and four tales, there remains the question of how fully its components are governed by this unifying pattern. For example, do the four pilgrims who tell the tales remain unaware of this theme, so that its strings are pulled solely by Chaucer? Or are we to think of this group of tales as a kind of debate in narrative form, with the four pilgrims recognizing and consciously answering one another's arguments?

I believe that we are to think of the Marriage Group in this last way, with the pilgrims carrying on a conscious debate or symposium. It seems to me, however, that the most convincing initial argument for a special relationship among these tales lies not in an interpretation of the tales themselves, but rather in the abundance of parallels and obviously pointed contrasts that exist among them. For example, all four tales tell stories that might be fairly summarized, "How two people got married and what happened then." Both the Clerk's Tale and the Merchant's Tale refer back to the Wife of Bath by name (IV, 1170, 1685). The Wife of Bath's views on marriage are contradicted directly by the Clerk's Tale, and more gently by the Franklin's later remarks on rulership (V, 761–770); and the contrast here is heightened by the contrasting theme of *gentilesse* in the Wife of Bath's Tale and the Franklin's Tale. The Merchant's Tale and the Franklin's Tale employ parallel casts of characters (the knight, his wife, and the squire who is trying to seduce her), in situations that are pointedly reversed: in the conventional Courtly Love situation of the Merchant's Tale, the lady has unwilling relations within marriage and willing ones outside it; while in the Franklin's Tale the lady

3. All quotations are from *The Works of Geoffrey Chaucer*, ed. F. N. Robinson, 2nd ed. (Boston: Houghton Mifflin, 1957).

has her Lancelot within marriage and is threatened by unwilling relations outside it. Both tales begin with long, static meditations on marriage itself—the Merchant's disillusioned and cynical, the Franklin's optimistic and serene. And both tales include gardens, apparently used with the same symbolic significance. A contrast of detail between the Clerk's Tale and the Merchant's Tale can be found in the descriptions of how Walter and January go about selecting their prospective brides—Walter by analyzing the virtuous character and behavior of Griselda (IV, 232–245), January by lying in bed with his mind like a "mirour, polisshed bryght" (IV, 1582), so that "Many fair shap and many a fair visage / Ther passeth thurgh his herte nyght by nyght" (IV, 1580–1581). Such parallels and contrasts among these four tales are in fact virtually inexhaustible, and cannot be convincingly extended to tales outside the group. I assume, therefore, that the four tales—along with the Wife of Bath's Prologue, which would be difficult to separate from them—are bound together also by some special thematic unity.

A part of our dissatisfaction with Kittredge's theory, I suspect, springs from the fact that the simple question "Who should rule the family?" is, taken by itself, the subject rather of television-drama than of great literature. I would suggest instead that the Marriage Group is organized thematically around a pair of intimately and complexly related questions: first, the question of which partner should rule, and second, the problem of the role of sex itself in marriage. The two can, of course, be connected to one another in various ways. For example, we may recall the fundamental division of the powers of the human soul into intellect and appetites (in broad terms, the "thinking" and the "wanting" parts of man) and observe that the problem of rulership involves a right ordering of the intellect, while the importance of sex is a problem involving a right ordering of the appetites. Again, it is worth noticing that on each of these questions, Christianity and Courtly Love stand squarely opposed. With regard to the role of sex, traditional Christian thought has always tended to subordinate the specifically physical in marriage (in the Middle Ages rather more so than now), while Courtly Love is based at least on physical desire, and usually on physical consummation or the hope of it. With regard to rulership, traditional Christianity emphasizes the authority of the husband, in accord with Ephesians

5:22, "Let women be subject to their husbands . . . "; and Courtly Love lays equal emphasis on the dominance of the woman, whose mastery is often conceived of as analogous to that of a feudal lord over his vassal. The most profound comedy in these two questions, however, springs from the fact that neither of them can really be disengaged from the other; tamper with either the physical relationship between a man and a woman or with the authority that exists between them, and both relationships are inevitably affected. The huge potential comedy of this theme rests ultimately, I take it, on a kind of built-in incongruity in sex itself—which seems to be the one human appetite intimately connected with both body and soul, and capable of ranging from the grossest physical bestiality to the highest spiritual sublimity.

In the Marriage Group, the underlying pattern seems to me to go something like this: Both man and woman want to rule. Man, who according to Christian tradition should rule, can manage to do so as long as physical relations are not placed too high on the scale of values. As they move higher on the scale of values, man's authority decreases and woman's increases. (Witness for example the Wife of Bath's dealings with her various husbands; and particularly the Merchant's Tale, where January's slavery to May's body eventually makes him a slave to May herself.) The further man's authority decreases and woman's increases, however, the more self-contradictory the sex-relation itself becomes—since, as we are constantly having to be reminded these days, man is supposed by nature to be the aggressor in such affairs. The Wife of Bath, for example, remarks concerning her five husbands that "thre of hem were goode, and two were badde" (III, 196). And so they were, with regard to her own ability to rule them—though it is impossible to miss the further implication that in certain other respects the first *thre* were very *badde* indeed, and the last *two* apparently quite *goode*. And at the end of her tale, the Wife's prayer for husbands both "meek" and "fresh abed" (III, 1259) leaves us wondering whether she is not petitioning Christ for a kind of minor miracle.

This whole relationship between authority and physical appetite can be supported also by the great biblical and exegetical symbol of the individual human being as a "marriage" of soul and body, with "man" represented by the soul and "woman" by the body. From this point of view, man's rulership would be

associated naturally enough with the suppression of the physical
appetites, and woman's with the dominance of the physical appetites. What finally emerges, I would suggest, is a complex "war
between the sexes," in which man's characteristic means of dominating is by direct exercise of authority, and woman's is by guile
in manipulating man's sexual desire. The two middle tales of the
group—the Clerk's Tale and the Merchant's Tale—present extreme uses of these weapons by each sex:

> In the Clerk's Tale, Walter's direct rulership over Griselda
> is employed fully and without restraint, to the virtual extinc-
> tion of her as a person.

> In the Merchant's Tale, May's sexual and other wiles are
> employed fully and without restraint, to the virtual extinc-
> tion of January as a person.

By contrast, the two end tales of the group—the Wife of Bath's
Tale and the Franklin's Tale—present more moderate and be-
nign rulership by each sex:

> In the Wife of Bath's Tale, the hag employs certain wiles
> both to catch her husband and to attain mastery over him.
> But as the tale is told, these wiles are clearly employed for
> his own good; and the final picture is one of female wisdom
> supreme, with man allowed his limited freedom within it.

> In the Franklin's Tale, as I read it, man's rulership is em-
> ployed to keep control over his wife, but indirectly and for
> her own good; and the final picture is one of male wisdom
> supreme, with woman allowed her limited freedom within it.
> (If this sounds like a gross misrepresentation of what actual-
> ly goes on in the Franklin's Tale, let me ask you to suspend
> judgment on it for the moment, and I will explain more fully
> when we get to it.)

With this general scheme in mind, let us now look more closely
at the components of the Marriage Group themselves. No one,
I suppose, is likely to overlook the many obvious charms of the
Wife of Bath's Prologue: her determined, if apparently rambling,
preoccupation with what might be called the anatomy of marriage; her strange and wonderful manipulations of formal learning; and particularly her gleeful acceptance of the concessions
granted to a physical existence only rather grudgingly by Paul
and Jerome. What has never been pointed out, I think, is the
precise way in which her Prologue is made to serve as an intro-

duction of the two large questions developed in the Marriage
Group as a whole. Underlying its apparent formlessness is a firm
and purposeful structure, with its major division marked by the
Pardoner's interruption: " 'Now, dame,' quod he, 'by God and by
seint John! / Ye been a noble prechour in this cas' " (III, 164–
165). Simply as spectacle, this confrontation of Pardoner and
Wife of Bath would be worth contemplating; our present concern
is with the fact that it divides the Prologue sharply into two parts.
Before the Pardoner's interruption, the Wife's monologue has
been primarily an evaluation of marriage, with particular reference to the familiar triad of virginity, widowhood, and marriage
defended by Jerome in the *Adversus Jovinianum*. Her whole debate about whether she is allowed to remarry is, of course, related
inevitably to this trinity of lives: is it to be continued widowhood
or reentry into marriage *for her*? Nor should one overlook the
comic appropriateness of her as a judge of the three ways of life,
since she is in a way the walking embodiment of them all—having
presumably been at one time a virgin, and subsequently married
and widowed five times. What is significant for our present purpose, however, is the way in which the whole question gets boiled
down to the surpassing excellence of physical union:

> Lo, heere the wise kyng, daun Salomon;
> I trowe he hadde wyves mo than oon.
> As wolde God it were leveful unto me
> To be refresshed half so ofte as he! (III, 35–38)

And again:

> In wyfhod I wol use myn instrument
> As frely as my Makere hath it sent.
> If I be daungerous, God yeve me sorwe!
> Myn housbonde shal it have bothe eve and morwe,
> Whan that hym list come forth and paye his dette.
> An housbonde I wol have, I wol nat lette. (III, 149–154)

In this first part of her Prologue, the Wife can in fact talk of
nothing else; and in the longer part of her Prologue following the
Pardoner's interruption (III, 188 ff.), her emphasis obviously shifts
to the topic of who should rule the roost. I conclude that the

governing design of the Wife of Bath's Prologue is as an introduction of the two questions I have proposed as the central theme
of the Marriage Group. With regard to the role of sex, she places
it unhesitatingly at the top of the scale; to the question of rulership, she answers with equal assurance that it should be seized
and maintained by the woman.

The Wife of Bath's Prologue is autobiographical, coarsely realistic, and apparently artless in progression; her Tale, by contrast,
is distanced in time, delicately romantic in setting, and highly
patterned in treatment. Its many-faceted theme, however, bears
on the same problems introduced in her Prologue, and produces
essentially the same answers. Most simply, of course, it can be
read as a sort of exemplum clinching her argument in the Prologue about female rule. We first meet the knight of her story
overcoming a woman, in a way that must be admitted to lack
something in finesse as well as in the general amenities of civilized
behavior. "Men," remarks the Wife in effect, "*are* beasts!" Then,
it has always seemed to me that there is a rather nice wit in the
queen and her ladies sending the young man out to discover
"What thyng is it that wommen moost desiren" (III, 905)—like
telling him, "Well, no, you've tried, but I'm afraid you've missed
the point. . . . Suppose you have another go at it and see what you
come up with this time." His search for the right answer, his
finding it, and his resulting involvement with a woman are, I take
it, a sort of fable of a young man's education in women and their
ways—or perhaps we should say the Wife of Bath's idea of a
man's education in women. At any rate, when the crisis comes
he makes successful use of his newly found knowledge that wom-
en desire most of all to have their own way; and the result is his
being overcome by a woman, but in a less violent and more
respectable way. "Women, on the other hand"—implies the
Wife—"are much nicer."

It would, however, be difficult to miss the further suggestions
of that significantly worded question, "What thyng is it that
wommen moost desiren." It is of course obvious that neither the
Wife herself nor the hag of her story would dream of being
satisfied with rulership alone; and there seems to be a further
comic hint in this same direction, in the fact that the queen and
her ladies evidently take a more tolerant attitude toward rape
than does King Arthur. Are we to understand, then, that the

knight of the tale—whose methodology admittedly leaves something to be desired—has nevertheless been on the way to one sort of "right answer" in his very preoccupation with passionate physical lovemaking? The successful answer given him by the hag—that women desire mastery over their husbands and lovers—certainly demonstrates that in one way or another she "knows women"; but one is left wondering in what way it manages to be the right answer. Is it simply the truth? Or is it rather what the hag knows the queen and her ladies will accept as the answer, in preference to a less decorous one? What emerges, I suggest, is an analysis of woman as governed not only by her desire for rulership over men, but also by her desire for sexual pleasure—a not altogether consistent pair, implying as they do a desire both to rule and to be ruled. This same analysis seems clearly extended to include the Wife of Bath herself, through her own ambiguous attitude toward her "good" and "bad" husbands in her Prologue, as well as by the implicit self-contradiction in her final prayer for husbands both "meek" and "fresh abed."

So far, I have said nothing about the hag's long sermon to the knight in the latter part of the Wife of Bath's Tale. There is, of course, a comic similarity between it and the methods employed by the Wife herself in improving her husbands; but its content seems quite foreign to the Wife's own views as they are announced elsewhere. The hag, you will recall, offers a spirited defense of her own eligibility as a lover despite her lowliness of birth (III, 1109–1176), her poverty (1177–1206), her old age (1207–1212), and her ugliness (1213–1218). There is some reason for suspecting that these four doubtful blessings are being pointedly opposed to qualities considered essential for success in Courtly Love, with particular reference to the famous De amore of Andreas Capellanus.[4] If this is so, there is surely a wry appropriateness in putting this criticism of an intensely aristocratic convention into the mouth of so blatant a specimen of the Middle Class as the Wife of Bath—the same sort of offbeat appropriateness, let us say, as there might be in having an arsonist express an enthusiasm for slum-clearance. Whatever the hag of her story may maintain, the Wife's own occasional comments on ugliness, poverty,

4. George R. Coffman, "Chaucer and Courtly Love Once More: 'The Wife of Bath's Tale,' " *Speculum*, XX (1945), 43–50.

old age, and lowliness of social station reveal small enthusiasm for them; in fact at one point in her Prologue, sighing wistfully over a happier past, she praises what appear to be their four direct opposites within a single line: "As help me God! I was a lusty oon, / And *faire*, and *riche*, and *yong*, and *wel bigon*" (III, 605–606). The comedy here, I take it, lies in the exact correspondence between the presuppositions of the earthbound and woman-dominated world of Courtly Love convention, and the earthbound and woman-dominated bourgeois world of Alisoun of Bath; and this correspondence, in turn, is based on their identical answers to the two questions which dominate the Marriage Group: woman should rule, and sex is supreme.

The Clerk's Tale, which is closely adapted by Chaucer from a Latin narrative of Petrarch, presents an initial dilemma of considerable complexity: does the emphasis of the tale fall more strongly on the individual story itself, or on what one is tempted to call its integration with the Group? If the former, we are confronted by the simple but genuine difficulty that most readers find the story at least partly absurd; and if the latter, we are left wondering why Chaucer saw fit to include Petrarch's moralization of it, according to which Walter signifies God and Griselda the faithful Christian:

> For, sith a womman was so pacient
> Unto a mortal man, wel moore us oghte
> Receyven al in gree that God us sent;
> For greet skile is, he preeve that he wroghte. (IV, 1149–1152)

A ponderous but convincing analysis by J. Burke Severs[5] has shown that the general effect of Chaucer's adaptation is to sharpen the story in all directions, making Walter more cruel, Griselda both meeker and more outspoken, Janicula more emotional, Walter's subjects more loyal, and so on. In addition, Chaucer seems to have been at some pains to emphasize both the literal tale and its allegorical significance, partly at one another's expense. For example, the teller's protests against Walter's injustice (IV, 456–462, 621–623)—the barest hint of which appears in

---

5. *The Literary Relationships of Chaucer's "Clerkes Tale"*, Yale Studies in English, 96 (New Haven: Yale University Press, 1942), especially pp. 229–248.

Petrarch's version—not only add to the emotional appeal of the literal story, but seem incompatible with its announced allegorical meaning, according to which Walter signifies God. What interpretation can account for this evident attempt to pull the tale in every direction at once?

I would suggest that within the context of the Marriage Group, Chaucer is deliberately highlighting the incongruity between the literal and allegorical meanings of this tale; and that the traditional allegorical meaning, carried over from Petrarch, here serves the unusual purpose of throwing critical light on the literal story itself. Walter, as the story is told, can signify God only by demanding for himself the kind of devotion which in literal terms the Christian can offer only to God; and in the same way, Griselda can signify the faithful Christian only by giving Walter the kind of devotion which in literal terms the Christian can offer only to God. So long as the tale is read allegorically, of course, these literal difficulties are not necessarily relevant; but in a tale told as part of a "Marriage Group," in answer to the Wife of Bath's literally told Prologue and Tale, they assume inevitable significance.

If the Clerk's Tale is to be understood in this way, with the emphasis falling primarily on its picture of marital relations, its answers to the two thematic questions of the Marriage Group will be obvious. To the question of rulership, the Clerk gives an exaggerated form of the traditional Christian answer that the husband should rule; and though his tale contains no explicit comment on the importance of sexual relations, their role—at least by comparison with the other tales of the group—is muted to the point where one hears of Griselda's children with something like surprise. The Clerk's "Envoy," for all its change of tone and skilful banter directed at the Wife of Bath, does nothing to modify this essential picture. As the Wife of Bath's Prologue and Tale present an archetypal woman's-eye view of marriage, with its contradictions presumably going over the teller's own head, so the Clerk's Tale presents an archetypal cleric's-eye view of the subject, with its essential naiveté at least partly lost upon its teller.

The last two tales of the group are told by a pair of laymen—the Merchant an embittered and insensitive man with a negative point of view, the Franklin a serene and penetrating man with a more positive outlook. Among the many devices used to point up the Merchant's insensitivity, let us notice for example the pseudo-delicacy which leads him unfailingly to comment on his own deviations from modesty, though always in a way that manages to underscore rather than diminish their effect:

> Ladyes, I prey yow that ye be nat wrooth;
> I kan nat glose, I am a rude man—
> And sodeynly anon this Damyan
> Gan pullen up the smok, and in he throng. (IV, 2350–2353)

As so often in the *Canterbury Tales*, however, the teller's lack of cultivation bears no relation to the actual handling of the tale, which is perhaps the most skilful and richly allusive of them all. Though this last claim has in fact little or no direct bearing on my present argument about the Marriage Group, let us pause at this point long enough to glance by way of example at the great image of the garden in the latter part of the tale—a symbol which, though it has been partly explained,[6] has so far received nothing like the attention its complexity deserves. For example, I do not think it has ever been suggested that so far as its biblical overtones are concerned, this garden seems to begin as a reflection of the *hortus conclusus* (or "garden inclosed") in Canticles 4:12, and to change gradually into a reflection of the Garden of Eden in Genesis; or that the climactic action in and around the pear tree then becomes an outrageous parody of the Fall of Man—with May enacting the role of Eve, and January's eyes opened so that he sees his wife, so to speak, naked. An illustration sometimes found in medieval *Bibliae pauperum* shows Eve actually sitting in the Tree of Knowledge of Good and Evil along with the serpent.[7] Both pear and pear tree are popularly associated

---

6. For example by D. W. Robertson, Jr., "The Doctrine of Charity in Mediaeval Literary Gardens: A Topical Approach through Symbolism and Allegory," *Speculum*, XXVI (1951), 43–45; Alfred L. Kellogg, "Susannah and the *Merchant's Tale*," *Speculum*, XXXV (1960), 275–279; Kenneth Kee, "Two Chaucerian Gardens," *MS*, XXIII (1961), 154–162; and Paul A. Olson, "Chaucer's Merchant and January's 'Hevene in Erthe Heere,' " *ELH*, XXVIII (1961), 203–214.

7. See for example *Die Darstellungen der Biblia pauperum in einer Handschrift des XIV. Jahrhunderts, aufbewahrt im Stifte St. Florian im Erzherzogthume Österreich ob der Enns*, ed. A. Camesina and G. Heider (Vienna: Kaiserlich-Königlichen Hof- und Staatsdruckerei, 1863), pl. I, left.

with lust[8] —so that one is tempted to see the pear tree in the Merchant's Tale as a little world of lust within the larger world of lust represented by the garden, which is itself part of the still larger world of lust embodied in the tale as a whole. However that may be, the repeated references to greenness in the latter part of the Merchant's Tale (IV, 2037, 2235, 2327, 2333) surely suggest cumulatively the traditional significance of green as carnality;[9] and the image of Eden is itself ironically anticipated earlier in the tale by at least six references—some direct, others more oblique—to the medieval commonplace comparing a happy marriage to the Terrestrial Paradise (IV, 1264–1265, 1331–1332, 1637 ff., 1670, 1822, 1964).

The Merchant's Tale is indeed saturated with traditional allusion of this kind, used with uniformly deadly effect. But let us return to our subject proper, and to the role of the tale within the Marriage Group. Clearly, it is the story of a marriage founded on little except male lust; and its answers to our two major questions are presented altogether by way of irony. For January, sexual pleasure is the supreme good; and as a result, his subjection to his wife at the end of the tale is complete. (As I read that ending, in fact, he is not so much deceived by May's explanation as he is unwilling to face the reality of what he knows he has seen, and so is reduced to the pitiful state of "believing" what in his heart of hearts he knows cannot be true.) For the disillusioned teller of the tale—of whom January must surely be taken as the thinly disguised *alter ego*—there can be no doubt about the present distastefulness of both these answers, based as they are upon his own bitter experience. The Merchant's Tale, then, presents in its way a less distorted view of marriage than either the Wife of Bath's Tale or the Clerk's Tale, but purely by negation. Whether the Merchant has any positive insights on the subject, we do not learn; that he knows what a good marriage is *not* is painfully clear.

Let me begin my discussion of the Franklin's Tale by suggesting that the uncompleted Squire's Tale which precedes it is not

8. See for example Olson, "Chaucer's Merchant," p. 207, n. 5; and Pierre Bersuire, *Reductorium morale*, XII, CXX, "De pyro," *Petri Berchorii Pictaviensis ... opera omnia* (Cologne: Joannes Wilhelmus Huisch and Petrus Pütz, 1730-1731), II, 513-514.

9. See for example Bersuire, *Reductorium*, XIII, iv, "De viriditate," ed. cit., II, 543.

"incomplete" in the usual sense of the word, but is represented as being tactfully interrupted by the Franklin in order to cut short a performance that might otherwise be counted on to extend to the crack of Doom.[10] The Squire, after 657 lines of an extraordinarily diffuse narrative, has just regaled the pilgrims with a preview of coming attractions:

> But hennesforth I wol my proces holde
> To speken of aventures and of batailles,
> That nevere yet was herd so grete mervailles.
> First wol I telle yow of Cambyuskan,
> That in his tyme many a citee wan;
> And after wol I speke of Algarsif,
> How that he wan Theodora to his wif,
> For whom ful ofte in greet peril he was,
> Ne hadde he ben holpen by the steede of bras;
> And after wol I speke of Cambalo,
> That faught in lystes with the bretheren two
> For Canacee er that he myghte hire wynne.
> And ther I lefte I wol ayeyn bigynne. (v, 658–670)

After such a forecast, there is surely some reason for asking whether the abrupt termination of the Squire's Tale a few lines later, followed by the Franklin's exclamatory "In feith, Squier, thow hast thee wel yquit" (v, 673), does not represent a tactful interruption of the tale by the humane device of smothering the teller with praise. And this conjecture is confirmed rather strikingly by a comparison with the ending of *Sir Thopas*, which obviously *is* interrupted by the Host. Both the Squire's Tale and *Thopas* break off near the beginning of an episode, shortly after the beginning of a new formal section (v, 671; vii, 891), and closely following a catalogue of adventurous tales (v, 661–669; vii, 897–900). Even more remarkable is the fact that both break off in the midst of a clause beginning with the word *Til*. The final lines of the Squire's Tale are "Appollo whirleth up his chaar so hye, / Til that the god Mercurius hous, the slye—" (v, 671–672). And the last stanza of *Sir Thopas* is as follows:

10. For a survey of similar opinions, see Charles F. Duncan, Jr., "'Straw for youre Gentilesse': The Gentle Franklin's Interruption of the Squire," *ChauR*, v (1970), 161; note also Joyce E. Peterson, "The Finished Fragment: A Reassessment of the *Squire's Tale*," ibid., 62–74.

> Hymself drank water of the well,
> As dide the knyght sire Percyvell
> So worthy under wede,
> Til on a day— (vii, 915–918)

These several parallels between the two endings suggest rather strongly that Chaucer found this a particularly attractive way of interrupting a tale; and that the Franklin's remarks following the Squire's Tale are therefore to be understood not as straightforward praise, but as a kindly stratagem:

> "In feith, Squier, thow hast thee wel yquit
> And gentilly. I preise wel thy wit,"
> Quod the Frankeleyn, "considerynge thy yowthe,
> So feelyngly thou spekest, sire, I allow the!" (v, 673–675)

I have dwelt at such length on this apparently tangential detail because if my suggestion is correct, it provides a preliminary glimpse of the Franklin as a man whose real point is apt to be a partially concealed one. This characteristic is revealed also by the well-known disparity between his disclaimer of rhetorical knowledge in his prologue (v, 716–727) and the highly rhetorical quality of the tale he tells; by the similar disparity between his later disclaimer of astrological knowledge (v, 1266) and the eleven lines of closely packed astrological description which follow almost immediately (1273–1283); and possibly by his announcing his tale as a Breton lay and making it sound in some ways like a Breton lay, though its antecedents seem in fact to be elsewhere. As we read the tale of this oblique-minded Franklin, then, it will be well to be on our guard.

The Franklin's Tale begins in a manner that seems to promise, if anything, a Courtly Love liaison:

> In Armorik, that called is Britayne,
> Ther was a knyght that loved and dide his payne
> To serve a lady in his beste wise;
> And many a labour, many a greet emprise
> He for his lady wroghte, er she were wonne.
> For she was oon the faireste under sonne,
> And eek therto comen of so heigh kynrede

> That wel unnethes dorste this knyght, for drede,
> Telle hire his wo, his peyne, and his distresse. (v, 729–737)

As a result of this service, however, the lady agrees "To take hym for hir housbonde and hir lord" (742), and the two pledge mutual obedience to one another in marriage (744–760). There follows an extended reflection on marriage itself, emphasizing the impossibility of rulership in love and the surpassing need for patience (761–786). The entire speech contrasts sharply with the bitterly ironic disquisition on marriage near the beginning of the Merchant's Tale (IV, 1267–1392); and in its emphatic combination of love and marriage, it is clearly intended to pick up where the Wife of Bath's Tale left off (III, 1066, 1091, 1230):

> Heere may men seen an humble, wys accord;
> Thus hath she take hir servant and hir lord,—
> Servant in love, and lord in mariage.
> Thanne was he bothe in lordshipe and servage.
> Servage? nay, but in lordshipe above,
> Sith he hath bothe his lady and his love;
> His lady, certes, and his wyf also,
> The which that lawe of love acordeth to. (v, 791–798)

It seems, then, that we have before us a story whose beginning situation is an attempt to combine what is best in Christian marriage with what is best in Courtly Love; and I have already mentioned the obvious reversal of the Courtly Love situation, with the lady actually married to the man she desires and almost trapped into compulsory extra-marital relations. If this is so, the beginning situation itself would seem to be statically ideal; and it might well be asked what creates the complication.

I would offer the suggestion that this combination of Christian wedlock and romantic love, though an admirable ideal, is in the nature of things an extremely difficult one to maintain; and that both Arveragus and Dorigen make the mistake of "overdrawing" a bit on Courtly Love behavior. Arveragus does so in behaving like a knight out of a typical romance and going off to "dwelle—a yeer or tweyne / In Engelond, that cleped was eek Briteyne, / To seke in armes worshipe and honour" (v, 809–811). We may recall that the hero of Chrétien's *Yvain* does this same thing, and with disastrous consequences for his marriage. Arveragus, by leaving his wife to her own devices for a year or two while he seeks glory in arms, creates a potential Courtly Love situation[11] —which in turn paves the way for her mistake. It begins with her going to the garden, which I take to carry the same general significance as the garden in the Merchant's Tale; and it is in this garden that the resulting bargain is to be kept. Once in the garden, Dorigen is subjected to the pleading of Aurelius. Her specific mistake is in answering him first like a dutiful wife, then like a candidate for a courtly amour (notice, incidentally, that she even gives him a task to perform), and finally like a dutiful wife again:

> "Is this youre wyl," quod she, "and sey ye thus?
> Nevere erst," quod she, "ne wiste I what ye mente.
> But now, Aurelie, I knowe youre entente,
> By thilke God that yaf me soule and lyf,
> Ne shal I nevere been untrewe wyf
> In word ne werk, as fer as I have wit;
> I wol been his to whom that I am knyt.
> Taak this for fynal answere as of me."
> But after that in pley thus seyde she:
> "Aurelie," quod she, "by heighe God above,
> Yet wolde I graunte yow to been youre love,
> Syn I yow se so pitously complayne.
> Looke what day that endelong Britayne
> Ye remoeve alle the rokkes, stoon by stoon,
> That they ne lette ship ne boot to goon,—
> I seye, whan ye han maad the coost so clene
> Of rokkes that ther nys no stoon ysene,
> Thanne wol I love yow best of any man,
> Have heer my trouthe, in al that evere I kan."
> "Is ther noon oother grace in yow?" quod he.
> "No, by that Lord," quod she, "that maked me!
> For wel I woot that it shal never bityde.
> Lat swiche folies out of youre herte slyde.
> What deyntee sholde a man han in his lyf
> For to go love another mannes wyf,

11. As an alternative, I suppose it is always possible that Arveragus' two-year absence is to be seen not simply as a mistake, but rather—or in addition?—as evidence of an unusual freedom from the kind of uxoriousness represented at the other extreme by January. Such a view would of course be more directly reconcilable with my suggestion about Arveragus' wisdom in the latter part of the tale.

That hath hir body whan so that hym liketh?" (v, 980–
1005)

Her banter about the rocks—besides being a symptom of her
genuine concern about her husband—is an attractive touch in
itself, intended to take some of the sting out of an otherwise
awkward refusal; but in an area of endeavor where "no" often
enough means "perhaps," and "perhaps" almost inevitably
means "yes," it will not do. Fired by this grain of hope, Aurelius
proceeds to accomplish the seemingly impossible and demands
his reward.

Now this error on the part of Dorigen is clearly part of a larger
theme in the Franklin's Tale, which, for want of a kinder term,
I suppose we shall have to call "feminine flightiness." Though
Dorigen is certainly one of Chaucer's more attractive heroines
and is portrayed with obvious sympathy, her intellectual powers
are not, I think, taken very seriously in the tale. The first hint of
this kind occurs shortly after the departure of Arveragus, when
the teller remarks of Dorigen, "For his absence wepeth she and
siketh, / As doon thise noble wyves whan hem liketh" (v,
817–818). A stronger instance is the passage in which Dorigen
solemnly undertakes, in good set philosophical terms, to explore
the problem of how the rocks along the coast of Brittany can be
reconciled with God's Providence (v, 865–893), ending with the
appealing but thoroughly unphilosophical conclusion,

> But thilke God that made wynd to blowe
> As kepe my lord! this my conclusion.
> To clerkes lete I al disputison.
> But wolde God that alle thise rokkes blake
> Were sonken into helle for his sake!
> Thise rokkes sleen myn herte for the feere. (888–893)

The fact that Dorigen does not ever bother to verify Aurelius'
news about the disappearance of the rocks (v, 1339 ff.) may, I
suppose, for all its contribution to narrative economy, be seen
also as a facet of this same characterization. In any case, after
Aurelius' announcement about the rocks Dorigen utters a long
lament, including an almost endless catalogue of ladies who sup-
posedly killed themselves rather than surrender their chastity (v,

1367–1456). This extended intrusion, so embarrassing to the narrative, is explained rather convincingly by James Sledd[12] as a comic device in which Dorigen's examples of "chaste ladies" become progressively less relevant as she proceeds, thus pointing up the limits of her capacity for rational analysis; and some such condescending attitude toward her seems implied also by the lines immediately following her lament:

> Thus pleyned Dorigen a day or tweye,
> Purposynge evere that she wolde deye.
> But nathelees, upon the thridde nyght,
> Hoom cam Arveragus, this worthy knyght. (v, 1457–1460)

—"and," I take it we are to add mentally, "she was not dead yet." A similar humorous condescension seems invited by her answer to Aurelius, when he meets her on the way to the garden and asks where she is going: "Unto the gardyn, as myn housbonde bad, / My trouthe for to holde, allas! allas!" (v, 1512–1513). To my ear at least, that second *allas!* makes this speech sound like nothing so much as the lament of a little girl who has just broken her doll.

But of course the climactic question concerning the Franklin's Tale is, What about the ending? Whatever interpretation we may care to propose for the tale, what are we to make of Arveragus' sending Dorigen off to sleep with Aurelius? I would begin by assuming that it cannot possibly be taken straight—that is, the point cannot possibly be that an unwilling act of adultery is somehow preferable to the breaking of a merely nominal promise. In Christian terms, even a genuine promise to commit a sin is not binding (though the promise itself would of course be sinful); and in the present case, Dorigen's remarks to Aurelius are obviously not intended as a promise at all, but simply as a graceful way of saying no. And according to any other way of thought that I can recall or imagine—including those of common sense and unprincipled hedonism—the keeping of this promise, in these circumstances, could be nothing but absurd. There is, I suppose, a theoretical possibility of taking it as simply a part of the fable,

12. "Dorigen's Complaint," *MP*, xlv (1947), 36–45.

serving the purpose of rhetorical hyperbole—as if to say, "So very great is the importance of keeping one's word, that *even if* this situation were to come about . . . ," and so on. But in questions of human conduct, such hyperbole can hardly be employed without itself becoming a false moral pronouncement, as it assuredly would here. Still another possibility might be to construe Arveragus' insistence on keeping the letter of the promise as some sort of satire on Arveragus himself; but this seems quite out of accord with the rest of the tale. What, then, is left?

It seems to me that Arveragus is being presented as an extraordinarily wise and idealistic man, who realizes that when Aurelius is confronted by this situation—that is, by a broken-hearted wife sent by her broken-hearted husband to keep a repugnant bargain—he will not have the heart to go through with it. The fact that the payment is to be exacted in a garden, in what seems to be the dead of winter, may be thought to present further complications; I read it as a symbolic reinforcement of the fact that in the present circumstances, the possession of Dorigen would be for Aurelius a merely technical pleasure. In any case, I suggest that Arveragus' sending Dorigen off to Aurelius is in reality a device to teach her a needed lesson in prudence, without letting her know that she is being taught; and that toward this purpose, he puts on a special act of sorrow for her benefit. When he is first informed of her predicament, his response is strangely serene and reassuring: "Is ther oght elles, Dorigen, but this?" (v, 1469). And a few lines later:

> "Ye, wyf," quod he, "lat slepen that is stille.
> It may be wel, paraventure, yet to day.
> Ye shul youre trouthe holden, by my fay!" (1472–1474)

What can be the significance of these lines, except to tell us that Arveragus sees further than we or Dorigen do at the moment? A little later, after Arveragus' sorrowful speech and Dorigen's departure (1475–1492), the teller himself intrudes with an even stronger reassurance concerning Arveragus' decision:

> Paraventure an heep of yow, ywis,
> Wol holden hym a lewed man in this
> That he wol putte his wyf in jupartie.

Herkneth the tale er ye upon hire crie.
She may have bettre fortune than yow semeth;
And whan that ye han herd the tale, demeth. (1493–
1498)

A passage like this, of course, effectively destroys whatever sus-
pense we may have felt about the outcome; and the teller's reassurance here is expressly concerned not only with the outcome
itself, but also with the wisdom of Arveragus in making this
decision.

One of my classes a few years ago included the proverbial
football player, who greeted this whole solution with the comment, "Well, you wouldn't catch *me* sending *my* wife off to no
garden on the say-so of no Averagius"—and I had to agree with
him: such dependable wisdom does not exist in life as we know
it. In literature, however—where characters can be more or less
symbolic in accord with the author's purposes—such wisdom can
exist, even in a character who has previously made the mistake
of leaving his wife for a year or two to go fight in tournaments;
witness for example Alyosha in *The Brothers Karamazov*, who can
be mistaken about the incorruptibility of Father Zossima's body,
but whose insight concerning Mitya's innocence is infallible.

This obliquity in the end of the Franklin's Tale, if it is plausible
in itself, will be quite appropriate to the character of its teller,
whose point, as we have seen, is apt to be the partly concealed
one. A similar obliquity can be observed in his final question,
"Which was the mooste fre, as thynketh yow?" (v, 1622)—a question which fits no interpretation very well if it is taken straightforwardly, but which under the present hypothesis becomes a device
for focusing our attention back on the supposed "generosity" of
Arveragus. "Do you see my point?" the Franklin asks in effect.
"Was he really generous, or was it something different?"

To whatever extent this interpretation of the Franklin's Tale
may be found acceptable, then, Arveragus becomes recognizable
as a husband who rules his wife not by dominating her, but by
outthinking her; and the ending of the tale becomes a precise and
meaningful contrast to that of the Wife of Bath's Tale—with male
wisdom supreme, and woman allowed her limited freedom within
it. Finally, what of the Franklin's Tale in relation to the two
pervasive questions of the Marriage Group? With regard to the

first, the role of physical relations is obviously neither exalted as in the prurient imagination of January, nor muted as in the Clerk's Tale; rather, it is emphasized in a few clear but discreet references, like for example the teller's exclamation, "O blisful artow now, thou Dorigen, / That hast thy lusty housbonde in thyne armes" (v, 1090–1091). The answer concerning rulership is more complex. Ostensibly, it is that of the Franklin's long early reflection: marriage is a mutual surrender of rights, and rulership as such has no proper place in it. The very action of the tale, however, with Dorigen throwing herself upon Arveragus' judgment as soon as a serious problem arises, seems to imply that in a crisis women do not really want to rule; and we have already noticed what I take to be its covertly undemocratic ending.

Though I suppose that the pictures of marriage presented in these tales may to some extent be taken as complementary, it seems to me that Chaucer's major emphasis falls finally on the Franklin's Tale as a presentation of the ideal, so far as it can be attained in a spectacularly imperfect world. Here as elsewhere, he seems to have had a positive phobia against getting the picture too neat; but if I am reading him correctly, the Franklin's Tale dramatizes what he takes to be about the best balance humanly possible between human love and the sacrament of marriage, between sexual pleasure and the less rapturous marital values, and between rulership by the husband and rulership by the wife. If we are inclined to be disappointed or skeptical about his falling back on male rulership after all, let us recall that it was a fundamental part of the very culture which produced him; and that not being neuter, he was unlikely to be altogether neutral. Even so, it is perhaps possible to put a slightly different edge on the interpretation I have offered for the Franklin's Tale, and to imagine Chaucer saying something rather more like this: "If man is indeed woman's intellectual superior—as Holy Church tells us, and as I duly believe—he will of course be able to stay one jump ahead of his wife, and to rule her the way Arveragus ruled Dorigen. Won't he?"

R. E. Kaske

Chaucer and
the Canticle of Canticles

The familiarity of medieval writers with the Bible and their pervasive use of traditional literary materials are undoubted facts. The assumption is therefore natural that the Canticle of Canticles—or Song of Songs—would be an important source of imagery and diction for medieval love poetry. Yet the direct influence of Canticles on the love poets of the Middle Ages is easily overstated, for in the works of many there occur virtually no clear echoes of the biblical love poem. Among secular love poets Chaucer makes some of the most notable uses of it; nevertheless, these are mainly confined to three works: the *Book of the Duchess*, written at the beginning of his career as author, and the Merchant's Tale and Miller's Tale, probably written toward the end. In his numerous important poems of love composed in the intervening decades hardly a hint of the biblical poem is heard. In order to understand Chaucer's uses of Canticles, and also why he and his fellow poets did not employ it more widely, it is necessary to review the exegetical and literary tradition of the biblical work. Consequently a substantial part of this paper is devoted to such a review, which includes consideration in some detail of several Latin poems.

For Christian theologians of the early centuries, the only way to justify the presence of an erotic epithalamium in the Bible was to find spiritual meanings for it. Carnal significance, as a result, was either denied to Canticles, or drastically subordinated to other meanings, and there emerged three full-scale spiritual readings that gained wide acceptance. These may be called the ecclesiological, the mystical, and the Marian, depending on whether the bride, or *sponsa*, is seen as the Church, the individual soul, or the Blessed Virgin. For the first two interpretations the commentary of the third-century theologian, Origen, provided the most potent model. He saw

Canticles as a marriage-drama about Christ and the Church on the one hand, and about the Word of God and the Soul on the other.

These were not separate readings. Rather, as Friedrich Ohly explains it, in Origen's view the individual Christian sees the marriage drama as expressing the mystery of the love between Christ and his Church, and he assimilates the drama to a personal experience in which his own soul is raised to discourse with God.[1] After Origen, too, there was no distinct separation of the ecclesiological reading from the mystical. For many centuries, nevertheless, particularly under the powerful influence of Bede's extensive exegesis, the Bride of Canticles was seen chiefly as the Church and quite secondarily as the perfected soul. And even after other readings became prominent, the ecclesiological remained important.

Only in the twelfth century, with the sermons of Saint Bernard of Clairvaux and his Cistercian followers and the commentary of William of Saint Thierry, did the mystical interpretation achieve independent importance. Bernard, while following Origen's lead, emphasized the mystical aspect much more, fully internalizing the drama, and seeing in the whole text the story of the coming and going of the Word of God in the soul.[2]

Full Marian exegeses of Canticles similarly were not composed till the twelfth century, though the interpretation of Mary as the *sponsa* had early origins in glosses of scattered verses by Ambrose and Jerome. Perhaps the most important stimulus to the Marian interpretation was the use of Canticles in Pseudo-Melito's sixth-century story of the Assumption. This use led to further references to the biblical poem in the tremendously influential letter on the Assumption by Paschasius Radbertus, long attributed to Jerome; it also led eventually to the incorporation of Canticles in the liturgy. The increasingly close identification of the figure of the Church with Mary was still another important factor among those that produced the exegeses of Rupert of Deutz, Honorius of Autun, Alan of Lille, and others, which interpreted the whole of Canticles as celebrating the mystical marriage of Jesus and his mother in the Incarnation and the Assumption.

1. *Hohelied-Studien* (Wiesbaden: Franz Steiner, 1958), p. 21.
2. Ohly, pp. 145–146.

Each of the three major interpretations—ecclesiological, mystical, and Marian—in the course of time resulted in the production of a variety of religious literature based on Canticles. The ecclesiological reading was the most productive of exegetical writings, but it was not an important stimulator of other literature. Most notable are some hymns written for the dedication of churches. The mystical interpretation inspired a more impressive corpus of writings of substantial literary value. The language of the biblical poem, for instance, pervades the works of Mechthild of Magdeburg and Richard Rolle, and is the basis for important mystical poems, including such fine Latin works as "Quis est hic qui pulsat ad ostium" and "Dulcis Iesu memoria," as well as the English "Quia amore langueo" and a number of the estimable poems in Spanish by St. John of the Cross.

The largest body of literature that utilizes Canticles is that which celebrates Mary, particularly her Assumption. Sequence upon sequence written for the Assumption and other feasts of the Virgin and based on Canticles may be found in Dreves's collections of medieval hymns. As might be expected, such liturgical works led later to the production of a substantial number of vernacular religious lyrics. For example, several English poems on the Assumption and Coronation of the Virgin in Carleton Brown's fifteenth-century collection are imbued with the language of the biblical poem.[3]

Secular works that use Canticles generally seem far removed from the world of serious religious writing. An understanding of the tradition of Canticles in exegesis and sacred literature nevertheless often contributes significantly to appreciating these works. Every poet of the Christian world had some knowledge of the tradition, and many, especially the clerical writers of goliardic verse, had a deep familiarity with it. Since the uses of Canticles by these writers are often related to the Assumption legends and liturgy, to understand the possible implications of their works it will be particularly helpful to consider the Assumption somewhat further before taking up several representative Latin secular poems.

---

3. *Religious Lyrics of the xvth Century* (Oxford: Clarendon Press, 1939), esp. pp. 65–70.

The Pseudo-Melito legend, and the Assumption stories which followed it, present two assumptions of Mary, the first being of her soul, which is taken up when she dies, and the second of her body, which is assumed after burial. The second Assumption is the more extraordinary so that the tradition focuses about this. According to this part of the legend, after Mary has been entombed, Christ and his angels descend to earth. He calls Mary from the tomb and kisses her. Then he and the angels take her up into Heaven where she is received with great glory.

The wording of Christ's summonses to Mary in the legends is related particularly to the biblical bridegroom's triple invocation to his bride, "Come from Libanus, my spouse, come from Libanus, come" (iv.7–8), and also his urging her to "Arise, make haste, my love, my dove, my beautiful one, and come." Versions later than the Pseudo-Melito make a great deal over Mary's reception into Heaven, particularly the angels' greeting her with "psalms, hymns, and canticles of canticles."[4] From this emphasis on music arise such pictorial depictions of the Assumption as the painting by the Master of the Saint Lucy Legend in the National Gallery, wherein angels playing a great variety of musical instruments welcome Mary into Heaven. As a result of Radbertus' sermon other texts of Canticles were early associated with the Assumption, notably the three "Quae est ista" questions, attributed to the angels of the legend who admiringly watch Mary ascend: "Who is she that goeth up by the desert as a pillar of smoke of aromatical spices?" (iii.6); "Who is she that cometh forth as the morning rising?" (vi.9); and "Who is this that cometh up from the desert, flowing with delights, leaning upon her beloved?" (viii.5).

With these several verses as a beginning, virtually all of the biblical love poem became opened to use in Assumption liturgy. Many of the Assumption hymns and readings reflect origins in the legend, and may be associated with events in the story. Thus an Antiphon for Vespers found in the York Breviary seems clearly designed as a speech of Christ when he descends to Mary's tomb:

---

4. *Apocalypses Apocryphae*, ed. Konstantin von Tischendorf (1866; rpt. Hildesheim: Georg Olms, 1966), pp. 128, 135, 117–118.

Thou art all fair, O my love, and there is not a spot in thee [iv.7]. Thy lips are as a dropping honeycomb: honey and milk are under thy tongue [iv.11]: the sweet smell of thy ointments is above all aromatical spices [iv.10]. For winter is now past, the rain is over and gone. The flowers have appeared; the vines in flower yield their sweet smell; the voice of the turtle is heard in our land [ii.11–13]. Arise, make haste, my love [ii.10]. Come from Libanus, come. Thou shalt be crowned [iv.8].[5]

Some longer liturgical pieces evoke a more complex situation. From an Epistle for the Assumption in a Sarum Missal of about 1300 we can postulate a very nearly complete Assumption drama. I have supplied the names of the speakers as I conceive the drama:

[Angels] Go forth, ye daughters of Sion, and see King Solomon [i.e., Christ] in the diadem wherewith his mother crowned him in the day of his espousals, and in the day of the joy of his heart [iii.11]. [Christ] How beautiful art thou, my love, how beautiful art thou! Thy eyes are doves' eyes, besides what is hid within [iv.1]. Thou art all fair, O my love, and there is not a spot in thee. Come from Libanus, my spouse, come from Libanus, come [iv.7–8]. How beautiful are thy breasts, my sister, my spouse! Thy breasts are more beautiful than wine, and the sweet smell of thy ointments above all aromatical spices. Thy lips, my spouse, are as a dropping honeycomb, honey and milk are under thy tongue; and the smell of thy garments is as the smell of frankincense. My sister my spouse is a garden enclosed, a fountain sealed up. Thy plants are a paradise of pomegranates with the fruits of the orchard, cypress with spikenard [iv.10–13]. The fountain of gardens, the well of living waters, which run with a strong stream from Libanus [iv.15]. I am come into my garden, O my sister, my spouse, I have gathered my myrrh, with my aromatical spices [v.1]. One is my dove, my perfect one is but one, she is the only one of her mother, the chosen of her that bore her. The daughters of Sion saw her, and declared her most blessed: the queens and concubines, and they praised her [vi.8]. [Angels, watching Mary ascend] Who is she that cometh forth as the morning rising, fair as the moon, bright as the sun, terrible as an army set in array? [vi.9]

5. Latin text in *Breviarium ad Usum Insignis Ecclesiae Eboracensis*, ii, Surtees Society, 75 (Durham: Andrews, 1883), col. 476. As with all English quotations of Scripture herein, the English version of the biblical passages that make up this antiphon is provided by the Douay translation of Jerome's Vulgate.

[Christ, now in Heaven] How beautiful thou art, and how comely, my dearest, in delights! Thy stature is like to a palm tree, and thy breasts to clusters of grapes [vii.6–7].[6]

This Antiphon and Epistle contain most of the major texts of Canticles that became associated with the Assumption.

From Carolingian times goliardic love poetry made considerable use of Canticles and its tradition, especially that related to the Assumption. The text of Canticles and the Assumption tradition are important, for example, in "Iam dulcis amica," a celebrated poem found in the tenth-century Cambridge manuscript as well as in two other versions. The poem begins with an echo of the bridegroom's invitation to his beloved to "Come":

> 1. Iam, dulcis amica, venito,
>   Quam sicut cor meum diligo;
>   Intra in cubiculum meum,
>   Ornamentis cunctis onustum.

[Come now sweet friend, dear to me as my heart; enter my chamber luxuriously decorated.]

In the two stanzas following he promises that the chamber will be hung with rich tapestries and strewn with flowers. The table will be laden with fine foods and clear wine; and, he goes on to say, there will be much pleasant music:

> 4. Ibi sonant dulces symphonie
>   Inflantur et altius tibie;
>   Ibi puer et docta puella
>   Pangunt tibi carmina bella:
> 5. Hic cum plectro citharam tangit,
>   Illa melos cum lira pangit;
>   Portantque ministri pateras
>   Pigmentatis poculis plenas.

[There sweet harmonies resound, and high-pitched flutes are sounded; there boy and skilled maid play for you lovely songs. He touches the cither with the plectrum, while she makes melody with the lyre;

6. Latin text in J. Wickham Legg, ed., *The Sarum Missal* (Oxford: Clarendon Press, 1916), pp. 308–309.

servants bring trays filled with cups of wine.]

The lover states that he looks forward especially to the conversation after the banquet, then renews his plea to his lady, his "soror electa," to come. She responds, it seems almost irrelevantly, by talking about her previous secluded life:

> 8. Ego fui sola in silva
>   Et dilexi loca secreta:
>   Frequenter effugi tumultum
>   Et vitavi populum multum.
> 9. Iam nix glaciesque liquescit,
>   Folium et herba virescit,
>   Philomena iam cantat in alto,
>   Ardet amor cordis in antro.

[I was alone in the wood, and enjoyed secret places; I often fled the tumult, and avoided crowds of people. Now snow and ice melt, leaves and grass grow green; the nightingale sings on high, and love burns in the recess of my heart.]

The lover does not respond directly to her statement, but rather concludes the poem with a plea to her not to delay.

> 11. Quid iuvat deferre, electa,
>   Que sunt tamen post facienda?
>   Fac cita quod eris factura,
>   In me non est aliqua mora.[7]

[How does it help, my chosen one, to put off what yet must be performed? Do quickly what you are to do. I cannot delay.]

---

7. The text of "Iam dulcis amica" that I have described and quoted is a standard composite of the three manuscripts. It may be found, for instance, in Helen Waddell, ed., *Mediaeval Latin Lyrics* (London: Constable, 1929), pp. 144–146. The manuscripts of the poem present substantial textual problems, even aside from the question of the last two stanzas. See discussion in Karl Breul, ed., *The Cambridge Songs* (Cambridge: Cambridge University Press, 1915), p. 92; also F. J. E. Raby, *A History of Secular Latin Poetry in the Middle Ages* (Oxford: Clarendon Press, 1957), I, 303–304.

He has suddenly become quite importunate.

Since the overtones of carnal urgency are not heard in the poem till the final two stanzas, I cannot share the amusement of Stephen Gaselee and Helen Waddell who smiled to find this lyric, in the manuscript version that lacks those last stanzas, in Dreves's collections of hymns.[8] Indeed, my supposition is that the shorter form was the original version and was written as an Assumption hymn, and that later a playful goliard added to the poem. This seems probable not only because the lover's attitude changes signally from one of gentleness and calmness to one of inordinate insistence, but particularly because the lady's words become understandable when imputed to Mary.

If one reads the work as an Assumption poem, the first stanzas can be interpreted as an address by Christ to his mother, inviting her to celebration and conversation in the *cubiculum* of the *sponsus*, that is, to the glory of Heaven with him. The emphasis on music—on the harmony of the flute, cither, and lyre—is quite in accord with the Assumption tradition. The lady's words in stanzas eight and nine, then, may be seen as a response by the modest and retiring Blessed Virgin, who shunned the world in this wintry life, and on entering Heaven finds winter past, the leaves green, the birds singing, and her heart on fire. Such an understanding of her speech conforms with Marian interpretations of the comparable lines in Canticles on the departure of winter: "For winter is now past, the rain is over and gone, the flowers have appeared . . . the voice of the turtle is heard in our land" (ii.11–12). I will quote on this verse only Amadeus of Lausanne, who is typical of the commentators in seeing the winter which has past as Mary's time on earth after the death of Jesus, and the spring as the time of her Assumption. Amadeus imagines Jesus speaking to Mary with these words:

Arise, therefore, my love, my dove, my beautiful and immaculate one, and come; for now the winter of my absence is past, the rain of your tears is over and gone, and the sun returning, the angelic flowers

8. See Waddell, p. 324.

appear to you. Your voice, O most chaste dove, has been heard. The time of the assumption has come.[9]

No secular interpretation of "Iam dulcis amica" accounts so well as a Marian reading for the lady's statement about the melting of snow and the coming of spring.

Her words in the same stanza about her burning heart, "Ardet amor cordis in antro," also may be connected with Mary's Assumption by way of another verse from Canticles. A quotation from Amadeus again will be apt. He here addresses Mary rhetorically:

> O Phoenix uniting all exquisite beauty! You are surrounded by a superessential fire as you fill with marvellous sweet incense the Heaven of Heavens and the angelic powers of Heaven. This incense is most sweet; artfully compounded, it proceeds from the censer of Mary's heart, surpassing in sweetness every perfume. At length the censer follows the incense, as raised by the hand of the Lord it ascends to the throne of God. It ascends surrounded by an escort of angelic spirits, who cry out in the heights, saying: "Who is she who goeth up by the desert, as a pillar of smoke of aromatical spices, of myrrh, and frankincense, and of all the powders of the perfumer?"[10]

The heart of the ascending Mary conceived of as a burning censer provides a neat explanation of the "pillar of smoke of aromatical spices" which ascends in Canticles. This gloss in turn may be used to explain the love burning in the recess of the beloved's heart in the Latin poem.

The addition of the final two stanzas, nevertheless, changes what is probably in genesis an Assumption hymn into a *carpe diem* lyric in which the lady is summoned to sensual love. The chamber of the *sponsus*, the flowers strewn on the marriage bed, the banquet, and the fine wine, all from the biblical poem, are put into the service of an urbane seducer. The bridegroom's characteristic terms of endearment, "soror electa" and "pre cunctis dilecta," assume a less elevating significance; and his imprecations to the bride to "come" and to "hurry," instead of being calls to a coronation, are exhortations to bed, motivated by an appar-

9. Amadée de Lausanne, *Huit homélies mariales*, ed. G. Bavaud, Sources chrétiennes, no. 72 (Paris: Éditions du Cerf, 1960), p. 200.
10. Amadée de Lausanne, pp. 178–180.

ent physical need that appears rather ludicrous, particularly in this context. Indeed, the whole of the lyric, when a carnal meaning is thus imposed, takes on the aspect of comedy. The lover's haste for physical consummation provides a humorous anticlimax to his previous dignified and elevated expression, and the speech of the beloved is made into the strange reflections of an inexperienced but willing country girl. The poet of the last two stanzas thus through the use of Canticles aims at light parody of the sacred epithalamium and its tradition, rather than any idealization of carnal love.

A less equivocal expression of concupiscent haste is found in another poem based on Canticles that appears with "Iam dulcis amica" in the Cambridge manuscript. The lady who speaks in this fragment is not trying to fool anyone:

> 1. Veni, dilectissime
>   Et a et o,
>   Gratam me invisere
>   Et a et o et a et o.

[Come dearest and visit me. I will be pleasing.]

> 2. In languore pereo
>   Et a et o,
>   Venerem desidero
>   Et a et o et a et o.

[With faintness I perish; I long for love.]

> 3. Si cum clave veneris
>   Et a et o,
>   Mox intrare poteris
>   Et a et o et a et o.[11]

[If you come with the key, you can soon get in.]

The tone throughout is playful, and the takeoff on Canticles provides straightforward humor. The poem uses once again the *sponsus'* call to his bride, "Veni, dilecta," putting it into the lady's

11. Reconstructed version from Raby, ii, 330.

mouth. It also employs a variation on the bride's "Quia amore langueo" ("For I languish with love") to express a purely carnal longing. And the last stanza exploits some of the possibilities for light innuendo presented by the bride's statement, "My beloved put his hand through the keyhole, and my bowels were moved at his touch," which is followed by "I opened the bolt of my door to my beloved" (v.4,6).

"Iam dulcis amica" and "Veni, dilectissime" were composed before the great mystical and Marian interpretations of the twelfth century. The partial defacing of these poems in the Cambridge manuscript may well have taken place under the influence of such devout and elevated commentaries; poems which profaned Canticles must have come to appear particularly sacrilegious. Yet it is clear that not all clerks of the later centuries had this pious attitude. The exotic language and the sensuous and often extravagant figures of speech continued to attract the goliards, almost irresistibly, it seems. One has only to inspect the thirteenth-century *Carmina Burana* to find large-scale utilization of the biblical love poem in secular works—for decorative imagery, for playful effects, and for downright parody. The frenetic gaiety of such a poem as "Veni, veni, venias" hardly disguises its mimicking of some of the best-known verses of Canticles:

1. Veni, veni, venias,
   Ne me mori facias!
   Hyria hyrie
   Nazaza trillirivos!

[Come, come, please come, do not make me die!]

2. Pulchra tibi facies,
   Oculorum acies,
   Capillorum series—
   O quam clara species!

[Your face is beautiful, the sword of your eyes, the line of your hair—O how your countenance shines!]

3. Rosa rubicundior
   Lilio candidior,

Omnibus formosior
Semper in te glorior![12]

[Redder than a rose, whiter than a lily, more beautiful than all others,
I ever glory in you!]

The triple call to come that opens the poem echoes strongly the
famous summonses of Canticles, discussed earlier. Linked with
the nonsense lines that follow, the humor is manifest which this
call to worldly love derives from its takeoff on Canticles and the
Assumption legend. The comic tone carries over into the subsequent strophes, which are also strongly indebted to Canticles.
While the echoes in stanza three are commonplace, stanza two
shows a more unusual debt to two different passages. The wound-
ing power of the lady's eye and hair implied in these lines is
explicit in the statement of the scriptural *sponsus*, "Thou hast
wounded my heart with one of thy eyes, and with one hair of thy
neck" (iv.9); and in the same lines "acies" (sword) and "series"
(line) recall the description of the bride as "terribilis ut castrorum
acies ordinata" (vi.9). The elevated images of the biblical poet are
converted into simple comments on the girl's beauty.

More blatantly profane in its parody is the poem "O mi dilec-
tissima!" which echoes two of the "Quae est ista" questions of
Canticles. A takeoff on the legend of the Assumption is implicit
in the questions in the poem:

> 2. "Que est hec puellula,"
> Dixi, "tam precandida,
> In cuius nitet facie
> Candor cum rubedine?"

["Who is this girl," I said, "so exceedingly bright, in whose face shines
white with the red?"]

> 4. "Que est puellula
> Dulcis et suavissima?
> Eius amore caleo,
> Quod vivere vix valeo."

12. *Carmina Burana*, ed. Alfons Hilka and Otto Schumann, 2 vols. (Heidelberg:
Carl Winter, 1941) i, pt. ii, no. 174.

["Who is this girl, sweet and most agreeable? I burn with such love for her that I scarcely have strength to live."]

In place of the angels' exclamations in admiration of Mary, the carnal lover expresses his lust at the sight of the *puellula*. The phraseology is almost wholly that of Canticles. The final stanza contains another use of the image of the maiden's locked door and the lover's key, and clears up any question about the lover's intent:

> 7. "Vellet Deus, vellent di,
> Quod mente proposui:
> Ut eius virginea
> Reserassem vincula!"[13]

["May God consent, may the gods consent, to what I have planned in my mind: that I should unlock her virginal chains."]

This goliard does not scruple to use a biblical metaphor to pray God that he may possess the virgin of his desires.

The poets of the *Carmina Burana* freely used the text of Christ's love song in secular poetry. Sometimes they used it merely decoratively or for light humorous effect, and at other times they openly parodied it. I think it important to notice, however, that there is a limit to their profanation of Canticles; they seldom, perhaps never, employed it in an attempt to idealize or spiritualize their ladies or their carnal passions. Their humor knew few bounds, it seems, but their romantic notions were strictly limited.

All scholars do not agree with me on this point. Peter Dronke, for instance, has thought to find elevation of physical passion in the goliardic works through the use of Canticles and other distinctively religious expression. He cites particularly the important "Si linguis angelicis" of the *Carmina Burana*. This poem of thirty-three quatrains begins with a famous line from Paul, and its second stanza starts with the opening of Fortunatus' hymn, "Pange, lingua." Though the subject of the poem is carnal desire and the satisfaction of it, these two tags from Christian literature are but the beginning of the poet's use of religious phraseology, especially of the language of Canticles and familiar Marian im-

13. Hilka and Schumann, no. 180.

agery and epithets. A summary will help to show the nature of the work.

"Though I speak with the tongues of men and angels," the poet begins, "I cannot express . . . how I am preferred ahead of all Christians." Then, of course, he proceeds to tell exactly how he has been honored. He relates that he was standing in a flowery grove, despairing of ever enjoying his love, when all at once he saw his lady:

> 6. Vidi florem floridum, vidi florum florem,
> Vidi rosam Madii cunctis pulchriorem,
> Vidi stellam splendidam, cunctis clariorem,
> Per quam ego degeram lapsus in amorem.

[I saw the blooming flower, I saw the flower of flowers, I saw the rose of May more beautiful than all others, I saw the brilliant star brighter than all others, for whose sake I had passed my time lost in love.]

> 7. Cum vidissem itaque, quod semper optavi,
> Tunc ineffabiliter mecum exultavi,
> Surgensque velociter ad hanc properavi,
> Hisque retro poplite flexo salutavi:

[When I had seen, therefore, what I always wished for, I was inexpressibly elated, and rising quickly I hurried to her, and greeted her on my knee with these words:]

> 8. Ave, formosissima, gemma pretiosa,
> Ave, decus virginum, virgo gloriosa,
> Ave, lumen luminum, ave, mundi rosa,
> Blanziflor et Helena, Venus generosa!

[Hail, most beautiful, precious gem! Hail, honor of virgins, glorious virgin! Hail, light of lights! Hail, rose of the world! Blanchefleur and Helen, magnanimous Venus!]

> 9. Tunc respondit inquiens stella matutina:
> "Ille, qui terrestria regit et divina,
> Dans in herba violas et rosas in spina,
> Tibi salus, gloria sit et medicina!"[14]

14. Hilka and Schumann, no. 77.

[Then my morning-star responded, "May he who rules the earthly and the divine, setting violets in the grass and roses among the thorns, be to you salvation, glory and healing!"]

The narrator-lover in these stanzas thus describes the girl with a string of epithets appropriate to Mary and indebted in part to Canticles: flower of flower, rose of May, bright star, morning star. Furthermore, he reports that he addressed her with a series of *Aves* and several more Marian phrases, notably "glorious virgin" and "rose of the world." As elsewhere in the poem familiar language of Canticles is echoed, at this point in the words which emphasize the lady's uniqueness, e.g., "cunctis clariorem", and in the lover's rising and hurrying to the lady, cf. "surgensque . . . properavi" ("rising, I hurried") with "surge, propera" ("arise, hurry"). The spiritual overtones of the stanzas imparted by such phraseology, however, are weakened by the lover's calling the lady by the names of two famous but human women, Helen and Blanchefleur; and the idolatrous nature of his praise is indicated by his identification of her with the pagan Venus. The lady's response further undercuts the lover's excessive praise by reminding him that in God, not her, lies health and salvation.

The lover, wanting the lady, not God, replies that she is his cure, since that which wounds is the best healer. In response she denies categorically that she wounded him, but she encourages him to tell his story on the chance that she might help. He then recounts the history of his love. Six years ago, he relates, he saw her at a dance; there she was a "mirror" and a "window" to all (st. 12). Both of these images have strong associations with the Virgin. He continues the story with several stanzas describing the lady's uniqueness and beauty: she was worthy to be venerated, "absque pari" ("without peer"), her visage was "clarus" and "splendidus". Again, however, he implicitly acknowledges his idolatry. "Oh God, my God," he reports that he asked himself, "Is she Helen or the goddess Venus?" (st. 14). He thus brings the story up to date. Continuing to use language characteristic of Canticles, he says to her that if she will now help him, "I will be glorified in you; as a flourishing cedar of Lebanon I will be exalted" (st. 23). She responds that she sees that he has suffered, and confesses that she too has suffered, even more than he. Then,

in a wonderful bit of mischief she deflates the praise that would
make a supernatural being out of her and of him a holy worship-
per. "Tell me, youth," she says (st. 26), "what you have in mind.
Do you want silver or precious jewels?" In other words, she asks
him to declare the real purpose of his high-flown language, which
she cannot take seriously. She knows, of course, what he is after,
and she evidently wants to oblige him, but she also wishes to draw
him away from idolatrous cant about the cedars of Lebanon. He,
however, is not yet ready to abandon his inflated sentiments:
"What I ask," he says, "gives easy solution to the impossible, and
bright joy to the sorrowful" (st. 27).

Her response to this at once expresses good-natured impa-
tience and expressly denies the supernatural nature he has imputed to her: "Quicquid velis, talia nequeo prescire" ("Whatever you
want, I cannot foretell it"). She disclaims prescience categorically. But now, no longer content with mere talk, with undoubted
irony she compromises her maidenly reticence and presents her
all to him: "Investigate sedulously," she instructs him, "and if I
have what you want, then take it": "Ergo, quicquid habeo, sedu-
lus inquire, / Sumens, si, quod appetis, potes invenire!" (st. 28).
This finally produces action. He rushes to embrace her, bestows
a thousand kisses, and receives a thousand in return. "Who," he
asks, "does not know all those things that followed?" (st. 30). He
concludes the poem by encouraging all lovers to persevere, which
coming from him is not without its own irony.

In concluding his treatment of the medieval Latin love lyric,
Peter Dronke discusses this poem at length; he sees it as a
veritable bridge between Latin and vernacular love poetry. He
states:

> In its high cult of the beloved, in its awe before the mystery of love,
> implying an initiated elite of lovers, in its extreme faith that love-
> longing and the lady together can realize a sublime ideal in the lover;
> in its hyperboles of grief no less than in its exultation, in its humour
> in the midst of seriousness, and its play on the profound paradoxes
> of love, "Si linguis angelicis" draws together some of the poetically
> most notable attitudes of the twelfth century *courtois* love lyric.[15]

15. Peter Dronke, *Medieval Latin and the Rise of the European Love Lyric*, 2nd
ed. (Oxford: Clarendon Press, 1968), I, 330.

This represents surely a serious misreading of the work, which is not about profound paradoxes, a sublime ideal, and an initiated elite, but rather is a witty tale of how an infatuated lover got his lady despite himself. The sublime ideal exists only in the deluded lover's mind.

"Si linguis angelicis" draws a large proportion of its phraseology and images from Christian sources, particularly from Marian literature. The poet, however, makes clear that the religious expression is not to be taken in earnest by putting it into the mouth of a lover who manifestly has fallen into idolatry. The depiction of such idolatry, of course, was not uncommon. Many poets wrote—often in the first person—about lovers who imputed supernatural powers to the lady and worshipped her accordingly. Generally, however, the language employed was more pagan than Christian, as in Chaucer's *Troilus and Criseyde.*

The situation and lovers of "Si linguis angelicis" have authentic counterparts in *Troilus.* Troilus is clearly idolatrous. He kneels down before Criseyde as before a goddess, and in bed with her he addresses a prayer to the God of Love, envisioning Criseyde as the god's agent in charge of him.[16] On Criseyde's part, while she listens to Troilus' long prayer and his protestation of faithfulness, she is "naught religious" (II, 759) and becomes somewhat impatient with his excessive show of piety when he carries it right into the bed. Your prayers are very well, she finally says, "But lat us falle awey fro this matere, / For it suffiseth, this that seyd is heere" (III, 1306–1307). The idolatry of the men in both poems is effectively counteracted and pointed up by the matter-of-fact attitudes of the ladies idolized.

The narrator and the lover in *Troilus,* to be sure, are separate persons as they are not in the Latin lyric. But Chaucer's narrator in Book III is every bit as idolatrous as Troilus, as shows up particularly in his comment about the joy of the lovers' first night together:

> O blisful nyght, of hem so longe isought,
> How blithe unto hem bothe two thow weere!
> Why nad I swich oon with my soule ybought,
> Ye, or the leeste joie that was theere? (III, 1317–1320)

16. III, 1291. Citations of Chaucer's poetry herein are from F. N. Robinson, ed., *The Works of Geoffrey Chaucer,* 2nd ed. (Boston: Houghton Mifflin, 1957).

Whatever foolishness his narrator speaks, one would not accuse Chaucer himself of being willing to sell his soul for the pleasures of love; likewise, it is not reasonable to attribute to the poet of "Si linguis angelicis" the same delusions about love that his lover-narrator suffers from.

In "Si linguis angelicis," then, the language of Canticles and other Christian literature is again employed for humorous purposes, not to exalt carnal love. In this case, however, the humor does not arise from parody of the religious texts quoted, as in other works we have discussed, but arises rather from satire. The object of the satire is the idolatrous lover, typical of many lovers of medieval lyric and romance. The lover's application to the lady of imagery appropriate to the Blessed Virgin simply demonstrates his befuddlement and foolishness. If the poem is at all autobiographical, then the author has a fine sense of irony about himself.

While, as we have seen, the writers of secular Latin love lyrics made substantial use of Canticles, the vernacular poets in all of Western Europe were more chary of using the sacred love poem, even to the point, one might think, of ignoring it. It is only by the broadest interpretation of Canticles influence that it may be seen as playing an important part in the vernacular tradition. It is true that Canticles in one place or another presents many of the common motifs of so-called Courtly-Love poetry—the *reverdie,* love-sickness, the description of the lady, the desire for a kiss, and so on. But it is far from being the only or even the major model for these. Neither the words nor the patterns of imagery of the vernacular poets generally indicate a direct significant borrowing from the biblical poem for such motifs.

When medieval vernacular poets do strikingly imitate the phraseology of Canticles, it usually indicates that the lady in question is seen as a being who transcends the carnal. This is the case with Dante's Beatrice who is summoned in the *Purgatorio* with the words, "Veni, sponsa" (xxx.11). It is also the case with the lady whom Guido Cavalcanti introduces in a sonnet with the question, "Chi è questa che vien, ch'ogni uom la mira?" ("Who is she who comes that every man gazes at her?"); the analogy with Mary's entrance into Heaven to the admiring gaze of angels evidently is intentional and seriously meant. The figure of Blanche in the *Book of the Duchess* is also depicted with the help of several more-or-less subtle uses of Canticles which aid in establishing another seriously-intended analogy with Mary, which I have discussed in detail elsewhere.[17] There are, however, two important instances in the vernacular literature of the Middle Ages when Canticles is used for comic effect. These are Chaucer's Merchant's and Miller's Tales. For most of the remainder of this paper I will direct attention to the part which the biblical poem plays in these two fabliaux, especially in the Merchant's Tale, since Robert E. Kaske's thorough treatment of this aspect of the Miller's Tale is well known.[18]

In both tales the clearest echoes of Canticles occur in addresses of fatuous lovers to their ladies. In the Miller's Tale, when Absolon salutes Alisoun while she is (unknown to him) in bed with Nicholas, his lines are a medley of the phraseology of Canticles mixed with his own foppish sentiments: "What do ye hony-comb, sweete Alisoun, / My faire byrd, my sweete cynamome?" he asks, and goes on in like vein for ten lines (I, 3698–3707). Kaske has noted several uses of Canticles in this speech besides the apparent borrowings of words and phrases like "hony-comb" and "sweete cynamome." And he points out that these lines present only the most obvious part of the comic parallel developed in the Miller's story. In the ensuing verses the contrasts between Absolon and the *sponsus* on the one hand, and Alisoun and the biblical bride on the other add to the humor right up to the climactic kiss.[19] The parallel, moreover, had been set up considerably before Absolon's speech, the portraits of both Alisoun and Absolon being well-laden with allusions to the descriptions of the *sponsus* and *sponsa*.

The correspondences of the Miller's Tale with Canticles extend quite far, and Kaske demonstrates that reference to traditional interpretations and associations often enrichens these correspondences. The use of Canticles in the Merchant's Tale is similar. There reverberations from the biblical poem spread out in both directions from the speech of old January summoning his young wife, "fresshe May," to play in his garden.[20] By making

17. I deal with the figure of Blanche in "The Apotheosis of Blanche in the *Book of the Duchess*," *JEGP*, LXVI (1967), 26–44, and in my forthcoming book in which I take up at length use of Christian analogy.
18. "The *Canticum Canticorum* in the Miller's Tale," *SP*, LIX (1962), 479–500.
19. Kaske, pp. 486–487.
20. The ironic relevance of this speech to the character of January and his cupidinous *hortus conclusus* is treated by D. W. Robertson, Jr., "The Doctrine of

use of the biblical bridegroom's call to his bride to "arise" and his triple invocation of her to "come,"[21] Chaucer divides the eleven lines of this speech sonnet-like into three tercets and a couplet. January begins with "Rys up," and at three-line intervals thereafter calls May to "Com forth":

> *Rys up*, my wyf, my love, my lady free!
> The turtles voys is herd, my dowve sweete;
> The wynter is goon with alle his reynes weete.
> *Com forth* now, with thyne eyen columbyn!
> How fairer been thy brestes than is wyn!
> The gardyn is enclosed al aboute;
> *Com forth*, my white spouse! out of doute
> Thou hast me wounded in myn herte, O wyf!
> No spot of thee ne knew I al my lyf.
> *Com forth*, and lat us taken oure disport;
> I chees thee for my wyf and my confort.[22] (iv, 2138–2148)

The circumstances of these "olde lewed wordes" and the use of the biblical poem have apparent similarities to Absolon's speech as well as some dissimilarities. Among the latter is the fact that January's words here consist almost entirely of direct quotations of substantial length from Canticles, rather than of the mixture of quotation, allusion, and personal sentiment found in Absolon's lines. January's effusion in fact could be used almost word-for-word as a reading or response in the liturgy of the Assumption, being made up of sentiments entirely suitable for Christ on his coming to take Mary to Heaven. Besides the call to the bride to arise and the threefold urging of her to come, there is an announcement that the winter of tribulation has past, a declaration of love-longing, and an invitation to her to come in her spotlessness to join her spouse. Indeed, the words that I imputed to Christ in the medieval Antiphon and Epistle for the

Charity in Medieval Literary Gardens," *Speculum*, xxvi (1951), 45.

21. The commentators almost invariably emphasized the bridegroom's three-fold repetition of "Come" in iv.8. See, e.g., Denis the Carthusian, *Dionysii Carthusiani Opera Omnia*, ed. Monks of the Holy Order of Carthusians, vii (Montreuil, 1898), 368.

22. Italics here and in subsequent quotations from the Merchant's Tale are mine.

Assumption quoted above contain virtually all of January's address to May. Chaucer no doubt carefully arranged the speech and consciously designed the parallel between the words of January and the Assumption liturgy in order to heighten the ironic contrast between the married couple's actions in the Merchant's Tale and those of the heavenly bride and bridegroom. The Virgin, "leaning upon her beloved," accompanies him to Paradise. May in the clutch of January goes with him to a Priapean Heaven.

January's building of a *hortus conclusus* and his long paraphrase of Canticles make the biblical poem part of the context of the tale; as a result, certain aspects of the story of May's adultery evoke some images from Canticles which have considerable potential for sexual interpretation. These involve the key and the door, the garden, and the fruit tree.

As we have had occasion to note, the lock and door are associated with images used by the *sponsa*. Though the medieval exegetes ignored the sexual implications of her words, we have seen two goliardic poems which demonstrate that the medieval reader with his instinct for analogy, no less than the modern seeker after psychological symbolism, recognized the parallel between the key and the door and the male and female sex organs. The lady in "Veni, dilectissime," for instance, tells her lover, "If you bring the key, you can soon get in." The sexual implications of the garden itself derive from verses in which the *sponsa* is represented as a garden bearing fruit: "My sister, my spouse, is a garden enclosed, a garden enclosed, a fountain sealed up. Thy plants are a paradise of pomegranates with the fruits of the orchard" (iv.12–13). The bridegroom's subsequent entrance into his garden (v.1) thus has implicit erotic significance. Finally, the bride even becomes the fruit tree which the *sponsus* desires to climb and partake of: "Thy stature is like to a palm tree, and thy breasts to clusters of grapes. I said: I will go up into the palm tree, and will take hold of the fruit thereof; and thy breasts shall be as the clusters of the vine; and the odor of thy mouth like apples" (vi.7–8). The sexual implications of these images could not escape the medieval reader; all are humorously relevant to the Merchant's Tale.

There are compelling indications within the tale that May, like the *sponsa*, not only is present with her spouse in the garden, but also in a sense *is* the enclosed garden to which January for a time holds the only key. Consider, for instance, how like his possessive fondness for May is his attitude toward the garden:

> This noble knyght, this Januarie the olde,
> Swich deyntee hath in it to walke and pleye,
> That he wol no wight suffren bere the keye
> Save he hymself; for of the smale wyket
> He baar alwey of silver a clyket,
> With which, whan that hym leste, he it unshette. (IV, 2042–2047)

He enters the garden whenever he wishes to "paye hys wyf hir dette" (IV, 2048). But May, we soon see, has no intention that January alone should bear the key to the door and garden that are so nearly identified with her person:

> This fresshe May, that I spak of so yoore,
> In *warm wex* hath *emprented* the clyket
> That Januarie bar of the smale wyket,
> By which into his gardyn ofte he wente. (IV, 2116–2119)

As the Merchant dwells on January's fondness for the garden, so also he makes considerable ado over the "clikets." Thereby he brings to the notice of his audience the symbolic potential of both garden and key.

May's imprinting of the key in warm wax is only one symbolic foreshadowing of Damian's eventual "thronging in." Immediately after January bids May, "Rys up, my wyf, my love," she signals to Damian, and in goes the key:

> On Damyan a signe made she,
> That he sholde go biforn with his cliket.
> This Damyan thanne hath opened the wyket. (IV, 2150–2152)

The entrance of the key into the door is followed by Damian's entrance into the garden, which also bears a symbolic burden:

> And *in he stirte*, and that in swich manere
> That no wight myghte it se neither yheere,
> And stille he sit under a bussh anon. (IV, 2153–2155)

In this garden that has virtually been identified with May, the bush that the lustful Damian, having entered the garden, sits under is surely figuratively related to May's pubic hair. In any event, there follows still another symbolic foreshadowing of the actual intercourse when Damian, like the *sponsus*, ascends the tree loaded with fruit:

> And with hir fynger signes made she
> That Damyan sholde clymbe upon a tree,
> That charged was with fruyt, and *up he wente.* (IV, 2209–2211)

He soon is enjoying the fruit he is looking for.

Chaucer's use of Canticles in the Miller's and Merchant's Tales certainly raises some questions about his attitude toward Canticles and indeed toward the whole Bible. For him to use one of the most revered books of the Bible for humorous purposes in his two bawdiest fabliaux at first blush seems daring, if not outrageous. Before hastily concluding, however, that Chaucer was an impious comedian, an apostate, or a liberated spirit in a shackled age, we must of course consider the direction in which the comedy of the tales cuts. It would be a mistake to see these stories as parodies of Canticles, that is as works which make fun of the biblical poem and its tradition as did some of the goliardic lyrics. Rather, the blade of humor slices in the direction of the characters and their behavior. Like "Si linguis angelicis," these tales satirize lovers typical of medieval romance and lyric. The biblical echoes show up Absolon, Alisoun, and Nicholas, January, May, and Damian as monstrous creatures who are ultimately funny in the same way as the grotesque beings who inhabit Hieronymus Bosch's "Paradise of Worldly Delights" are funny. As D. W. Robertson, Jr., remarks of the scriptural echoes in January's speech, "They show the extreme foolishness to which cupidity like January's may lead. For the doting knight, May represents what the lady in *Canticum* represents to the faithful: she is his Holy Church, his Blessed Virgin, his refuge from the transitory world."[23] Kaske similarly states, while properly asserting the effectiveness of the Miller's Tale as comedy, "In the Miller's Tale,

23. Robertson, p. 45.

the accumulated echoes from the *Canticum* seem to me to produce a riotous though meaningful contrast between the *caritas* to which the Sponsus-Christ allegorically exhorts the sponsa-Church, and the quite different attraction which literally motivates Absolon's exhortations to Alisoun."[24] More specifically he suggests, "Perhaps even the full comic incongruity of the 'sponsa' Alisoun (centered in the awkward question of whose sponsa she really is) presupposes a spontaneous unobtrusive awareness of the sublime incongruity of Mary, the sponsa wholly without knowledge of man—a possibility that is certainly not diminished by Alisoun's role as 'carpenteris wyf.' "[25]

The ironic disparity between the lovers in the two fabliaux and Christ and Mary is heightened by each detail of the parallels that are implicitly drawn. Every echo of Canticles emphasizes the contrast between the carnal reality portrayed in the tales and the spiritual ideal that was found to be expressed in the Bible. Alisoun's breath, apple-sweet like the biblical bride's, belies her corruption; Absolon's hair, which like that of the *sponsus* resembles the branches of palm trees, matches his effeminate vanity with the virile dignity of the bridegroom; and the *sponsus*' exciting call to love, Christ's call to Mary in the legend of the Assumption, assumes in January's mouth the sense and savor of the bleat of a lecherous goat. These characters cannot make Canticles a comic discourse; they can only make themselves grotesque.

Witness the amusing, disgusting spectacle which Damian and May make of themselves when they act out their version of the *sponsus*' words: "I will go up into the palm tree, and will take hold of the fruit thereof; and thy breasts shall be as the clusters of the vine" (vi.7–8). Denis the Carthusian comments on this verse, "If by the palm is understood the most illustrious Virgin, it signifies that the only-begotten Son of God, through the mystery of his incarnation descends into her and takes her fruits. . . . If again by the palm is understood the cross of the Saviour, this the most worthy Mother assuredly ascended by desire with her son, and by most worthy imitation and the greatest compassion."[26] It is the Incarnation and the Crucifixion that Damian and May portray as an absurd comedy of lust. This can but reflect on them.

24. Kaske, p. 480.
25. Kaske, p. 497.
26. *Opera Omnia*, vii, 428.

In medieval secular love poetry, the notable uses of Canticles are in general confined to three literary classifications: Latin goliardic lyrics, *dolce stil nuovo* and comparable poetry in which the lady is spiritualized, and Chaucer's two fabliaux. Probably because of the almost exclusively spiritual interpretation of Canticles, the vernacular poets did not usually find their subject matter compatible with Canticles. They did not use Canticles to impute spirituality to a love that was primarily carnal, nor to blur the distinction between carnal and heavenly love. Thus it is not accurate to say that the phraseology employed in secular and religious poetry of love in the Middle Ages is interchangeable. In certain kinds of religious poetry the conventional language of Courtly Love is indeed very common, but the reciprocal use in secular works of characteristically Christian expression, such as the words of Canticles and Marian imagery, has definite limits. Chaucer's three major uses of Canticles in his works accurately reflect these limits.

James I. Wimsatt

Panel Discussion

MODERATOR: Edgar H. Duncan

PANELISTS: Norman E. Eliason, Robert E. Kaske, Edmund Reiss, James I. Wimsatt

DUNCAN   I propose that in the fifty minutes remaining we have as many questions from the audience as we can entertain. And I suggest that, since we have already heard at length from the four gentlemen, the discussion among them be somewhat curtailed so that we can have more questions from the audience. I want first to give my impressions of the proceedings thus far, with the hope that they will set the discussion going among the panelists. It seems to me that the four papers on Chaucer the love poet have demonstrated that love is, as I am sure someone has said, a many-splendored thing, and that Chaucer's uses of the themes and language of love are of a variety that approaches infinity. More particularly, Mr. Eliason would convince us that in reading Chaucer's love poems what you see is what is there, but that much modern scholarship seems designed to consist of red herrings to divert the reader from looking at what is there. I would say that Mr. Reiss maintains with equal cogency, on the other hand, that what is there is merely a hint—and sometimes a quite tantalizingly vague hint—of what one *should* see there. In the third place Mr. Kaske avers that on the subject of love in marriage, as perhaps on all other subjects, Chaucer plays games with us and that our fun is in our playing the games after him, with the added observation that Chaucer's games always come out right (women's lib notwithstanding)—that they are games, not tricks. And finally Mr. Wimsatt has shown that behind Chaucer's use of amatory language for romantic or comic effect lies a tradition rich in its medieval development, and that Chaucer's originality consists in his unique appropriation of that tradition. Now anyone's summation of these four rich papers would be open to question, of course, and I perhaps can begin the discussion by asking our panelists if they will comment on these four statements.

ELIASON   Well, I hadn't quite intended to say that the other three speakers are mere red herrings that are gumming up the works, so to speak. I tried to make the point that indeed we have to know about medieval love, the strange kinds of love—the kinds of love, for example, that Mr. Wimsatt was speaking of at the end, and the kinds of love that Mr. Reiss was speaking of as being contained in the first group of tales, and the kind of love in the two themes of sex and *maistrie* (question of who is to be boss) that Mr. Kaske analyzed in the so-called Marriage Group—we have to know about these things. But the question still remains, it seems to me, whether Chaucer has anything to say today, to people who read him, about the kind of love still of interest to us now. In that sense I suppose I feel that there is a little red herring business going on—that because of it we get distracted, we get so enthralled in the use, for example, of Canticles through the Middle Ages in these strange ways, in these impious ways, we get so enthralled by it, that when we come to Chaucer and look, for example, at that notable use of the Canticles in the Merchant's Tale, we hardly know what to think. Mr. Wimsatt made a point of this. He said some questions are naturally raised. The crucial question here, it seems to me, is this: is Chaucer a mischievous, an impious fellow—very mischievous, very impious? I think not. Mr. Wimsatt pointed out that really what Chaucer is using Canticles for in the Merchant's Tale (and this holds true in the Miller's Tale), is to demonstrate (if we don't already know it) what both of these people are—to demonstrate that January is a fool and to demonstrate that Absolon is an ass. We have notice of that beforehand. But when Absolon speaks as he does out there at the window, then any conceivable doubts about it vanish. And we laugh and we are supposed to laugh at that. We're not supposed to scratch our heads and say, "Good heavens, is Chaucer headed for hell because of his mischievous use of Canticles?" I don't read the thing that way. And then of course I don't go on to read with Mr. Wimsatt some further implications there. If Alisoun is to be equated with the Virgin, then Chaucer becomes impious in a way that I don't see. That's not red herring; that's just wrong.

With Mr. Kaske's paper—I'm more familiar with that—I've heard it once before. Well, only once, and it bears rehearing. In fact I enjoyed it very much more this time than I did the first time, and you will have the same experience. I was particularly pleased there with what he did with the Squire's Tale. This has nothing to do with love, but it's the best thing I know on the Squire's Tale—the first time someone has zeroed in and said, "Well of course this silly thing is ended and ended when it should be; we've had enough of it."

Mr. Kaske and Mr. Reiss and Mr. Wimsatt *all* center attention on one small part of Chaucer. Now the Marriage Group isn't too small, I grant that; nor is the first group of tales too small, I grant that; nor are these passages in the two tales mentioned too small. My appeal, however, is to look at all of Chaucer. If we want to see him as a love poet—and that is the theme of the conference, I remind you—then we need to read all of Chaucer and see if he is discussing love there and discussing it in a way of interest to us today, of interest even to Ann Landers. The interest resides in this simple question: what is it that happens when a man meets a girl and they fall in love? Neither the question nor the various answers Chaucer provides require any vast erudition to understand. In his love poetry it seems to me that Chaucer has come to grips with some very basic things and said them very well. Therefore it is all of Chaucer's poetry, not just some small part of it, that I would want to look to.

WIMSATT Well, I've learned a lot from listening to the papers. What Mr. Eliason has to say, of course, is ringing in my ears most immediately. I was thinking that when he refers to Ann Landers, I guess he could hardly pick out a more antiromantic person to refer to.

ELIASON She's from my wife's home town; that's why she came in.

WIMSATT She, like Chaucer, has a certain moral attitude towards love. If some girl writes and says, "Oh, I've fallen in love with this boy and would it be all right if we do so and so?" then Ann Landers says "No!" Her advice to Criseyde would certainly stop the story short at some early point. I think that Chaucer has a moral attitude that is reflected in his love poetry, just as Ann Landers has an attitude that's reflected in her columns, and that Chaucer's attitude is also ultimately antiromantic. Though he sets up a romantic narrator in *Troilus and Criseyde*, this narrator looks foolish, is purposely made to look foolish, as notably in the example I cited where the narrator wishes he had sold his soul for just one of the least joys of that night. And the attitude, of course, is effectively asserted at the end—Chaucer's Christian attitude is effectively asserted at the end, with the retraction. I think that what interests me most about Chaucer's love poetry—of course I enjoy his depictions of love for themselves—but what I most enjoy is seeing how Chaucer asserts ultimately a moral attitude in his love poetry, an attitude that perhaps is a little bit too rational for today's romantics. Mr. Eliason I think rightly said that Chaucer is an intellectual poet, and he deals with love in a way that is intellectual. Of course this agrees fairly closely with what Mr. Reiss asserted about Chaucer's parodies. In a Christian sense, I suppose with what Mr. Reiss calls parodies you always have in mind the contrast of that which should be as contrasted with that which is—the contrast may be presented in a quite muted fashion in *Troilus and Criseyde*, but in the fabliaux I think it is presented very strongly. And I think that this is what we need to have pointed out to us.

With Mr. Kaske's paper (this is the first time I've heard it—I've heard *about* it), I was very curious as to what he would have to say about the Franklin's Tale, because I've never been satisfied with any of the explanations that have been offered one way or another about its conclusion; and I would say that if there is a solution, Professor Kaske's is no doubt it. And I was pretty well convinced by the presentation.

REISS Mr. Eliason's words reminded me of an old colleague of mine who was talking to an undergraduate having difficulty writing a term paper on *Hamlet*, and finally in desperation my colleague said to this student (who wasn't a very good student), "Well, write about what *Hamlet* means to you, in your life in your fraternity." I suppose it would have been amusing to see the results of that. I do think that we all are implicitly concerned with what any writer we read does for or means to us. At the same time we detach ourselves from the work, saying, I'm interested in seeing what this writer is doing himself, what his works mean themselves—what Henry James called giving the writer his *don-née*. I would like to see what Chaucer's *donnée* is. Often this means artificially going through a process that perhaps ruins the joke for some people. All spelling out tends to do this sort of thing. It's unfortunate that scholarship involves spelling out. I've often wondered how someone five hundred years from now would respond to the television program "Laugh-In." What kind of spelling out of those jokes would be necessary? So we spell things out at the same time as we wish we didn't have to. Hopefully, after we spell it out, we can then go back to the work and say all this is incorporated in it, and here's what the work is doing in toto.

I think that this program has brought out various ways Chaucer uses love, various levels of his use of love, and various approaches to Chaucer. I was delighted with the way in which we all seemed to concentrate on different aspects of it, and yet there was a kind of dovetailing in what we were doing. Rather than say that one approach is wrong, I would say that one approach will look at something and perhaps miss certain other things that are in the work. I'm sure my approach does this too. The ideal approach is that which takes everything into account and understands it. That at least is the most satisfying. The nice thing about scholarship—and the frustrating thing—is that apparently none of us at any one time is able to see the entire picture at that moment. Such, I suppose, justifies the very existence of conferences like this.

KASKE   I would just like to make one small, suggested addition to Professor Wimsatt's brilliant treatment of Chaucer's use of Canticles—I can't praise this paper highly enough. I find myself wondering whether in the General Prologue, the description of the Pardoner, "Ful loude he soong 'Com hider, love, to me!' " is not a further echo of the Canticles—echoing the repeated "Veni, veni, amica mea" that comes up over and over again in various forms in Canticles. It would work so nicely there, because here is the Pardoner who is physically crippled as we know, or physically lacking, let us say, and if this is an echo of Canticles it would contribute to this physical deformity of the Pardoner's as a symbol of a spiritual deformity, you see. I think it would have that very powerful force, particularly if, as I certainly believe, the Pardoner is being presented as the homosexual companion of the Summoner—"This Somonour bar to hym a stif burdoun," which means ground melody, but a burdoun is also a very suggestively shaped staff with an iron tip. I think it speaks for itself. If this is so, if "Ful loude he soong 'Com hider, love, to me!' " is a further echo of Canticles, isn't it remarkable how in his mature works Chaucer has chosen to put echoes of Canticles into the mouths of precisely this trio of lovers: the Pardoner, Absolon, and January, all of them futile lovers. He obviously finds Canticles a very potent vehicle for this kind of ironic or slanted judgment in his mature works. The *Book of the Duchess* is of course the exception to this.

DUNCAN   We're ready now for questions from the floor.

QUESTION   I would like to ask Mr. Wimsatt, since the Canticle of Canticles had difficulty getting into the canon despite the allegorical interpretation, I wonder if, despite the reverence in which tales of the Assumption were held, the literate man of the Middle Ages might not have been aware of the potentiality of the Canticles as amorous—as *merely* amorous love poetry, and how this would affect his interpretation?

WIMSATT   The question of the admission of Canticles into the canon was of course resolved very early, so that this would not have been reflected any time, surely, after the tenth century. The interpretations—the spiritual interpretations—of it, of course, before the twelfth century were fairly common, and they were strong in asserting the spirituality of the Canticles. And after the twelfth century, because of Bernard particularly—his sermons being very well known, and of course many other like interpretations having currency—I think that the secular poets clearly shied away from it. And this is one point that I was trying to make in my paper—that you don't find very important, serious uses of it in vernacular poetry. The Latin goliards were willing to use it *despite* their knowledge, their familiarity with the tradition; but the secular, vernacular poets just wouldn't presume to use it, as far as I can see. This indicates to me a very strong consciousness of the spiritualization of Canticles, the denial of the carnal sense, which Bernard emphasizes time and again in his sermons to the monks.[1] Bernard is very worried that the monks are going to get some amorous ideas out of the Canticles. Clearly his worry, his concern, was justified: the goliards found plenty of amorous ideas, as would anybody who reads it, I suppose.

DUNCAN I would like to ask a corollary to this. What do you say about Chaucer's intention? If he is the only one, so far as you have found, in medieval vernacular literature who makes such extreme use of Canticles, in such a farcical or humorous—whatever you want to say—ludicrous way, was he being daring—or what *was* he being?

WIMSATT I think probably he felt his own competence, and like Dante or Langland he was willing to be daring in his uses of Canticles.

DUNCAN Would you add also that he realized he was writing for, and, in so far as he delivered these things in person, reading them before a very sophisticated audience?

WIMSATT Yes, that sounds right to me. But perhaps Professor Kaske would comment on that, since he is quite an expert on this subject.

KASKE I have to disclaim that. Jim Wimsatt has gone much further by now in this subject than I ever did. But yes, it seems to me from what I know about it that through the Middle Ages one of the attractive things about Canticles is this tension that exists between the literal reading (which obviously on that level is a very erotic poem indeed) and the spiritual meanings. It seems to me that this gives a poet like Chaucer endless opportunities for playing around with it, in a kind of grinning way, playing on both levels at once. Isn't this right, Jim—some of the medieval exegetes do put emphasis also on the literal level without ever denying the

1. For instance in one sermon he admonishes them, "Bring modest ears to the text of love we have in hand. When you think of the lovers, it is necessary that you think not of a man and woman, but of the Word of God and the Soul." See Sermon LXI, 2, *Sermones Super Cantica Canticorum*, ed. J. Leclerq et al., in *Sancti Bernardi Opera*, II (Rome: Editiones Cistercienses, 1957–1958).

spiritual level? It seems to me that Robertson in *Preface to Chaucer* cites Nicholas de Gorran to that effect. Am I remembering that right?

WIMSATT   Honorius of Autun is the one I know.

KASKE   I think that there is a passage also in Nicholas de Gorran, in which he is quite frank about—"Yes, isn't this a fine erotic love piece? Not for everyone, of course!"—but then of course proceeds to give the spiritual reading too.[2] This I suppose is a kind of additional answer to the gentlemen who was asking that question a moment ago.

QUESTION   I would like to ask a question about the dovetailing of the papers which Mr. Reiss mentioned. If I'm not mistaken, Mr. Kaske has left us with May up a tree as Eve with the serpent Damian, and Mr. Wimsatt left us with May up a tree as Mary with the *sponsus* Damian. We know that religion and love are both very full of paradoxes, and I wondered if the panelists could resolve the paradox.

KASKE   I would reply that you are accurate enough in a general way, but it's subtly inaccurate. When you say that May is up a tree *as* Eve, there's already a little more direct and, oh, one-for-one correspondence than I intend. I suspect this is true of Jim also. I'd say there is what I'd call a hovering correspondence or a hovering overtone. We are meant to be unobtrusively reminded of Eve. I wouldn't claim anything like an allegorical or symbolic correspondence. It's closer to analogy—see what I mean?—rather than May up the tree standing *for* Eve. She is meant momentarily to remind us of Eve; Eve is meant to flicker across our imagination at this point. If it operates that way, then so far as the doubleness of the reference goes I think there's no problem. After all, Eve and the Virgin Mary are notorious antitypes, aren't they? And I think there's no reason why May up the tree could not remind us in this way—well, May would remind us *directly*

2. Actually, as Mr. Kaske pointed out later, the passage which he was trying to recall was not by Nicholas but by Gilbert of Hoiland, quoted in D. W. Robertson's *A Preface to Chaucer* (Princeton: Princeton University Press, 1963), p. 135.

of Eve; she would remind us *per antiphrasim*, as they say, of the Virgin Mary. That's how I would work it out.

WIMSATT   It seems to me that we do have a case of analogy here and the number of potential analogies is almost limitless. Of course, the garden is specifically, explicitly compared by Chaucer to the garden of Priapus, to the enclosed garden of Canticles, to Eden, to Olympus. Other analogies are perfectly possible within this many-splendored garden.

REISS   Of course, the whole doctrine of recapitulation goes back as far as Irenaeus, and I guess the whole Mary-Eve parallel was stated first by Justin Martyr back in the second century. From that time on it's the whole idea of renewal that's being brought out by Mary; and, of course, the obvious result of this here is January's gaining his sight again—being able to see—and we have a new beginning again.

QUESTION   I would like to ask Professor Kaske, in light of what has been said about analogy, could we then move on into *Troilus and Criseyde* and say that Troilus and Criseyde in bed with Pandarus nearby might be compared with Adam and Eve in Paradise and Pandarus as the devil?

KASKE   Well, I hadn't thought about it. I would say that any analogy of this kind depends on specific recognizable correspondences. After all, Chaucer, if he intends analogies of this kind, must have been faced with approximately the same problem in getting them across to his original audience as he is to us. I'm sure they were familiar with medieval lore in a way we are not, but still it's essentially the same problem—he would have to put up signposts. I would ask, if someone proposed this to me, what signposts do you find? As you put it, I don't see any. There may be more specific things that would flesh it out, make it credible.

REISS   Pandarus as devil figure, of course, is brought out, and there are references to hell throughout that whole scene.

QUESTION   I'd like to ask a question of a more generic sort. Professor Eliason mentioned something about tone. How do we interpret tone in earlier poetry? It has been shown that the tone we moderns hear in the line from *Cymbeline*—"Golden lads and girls all must as chimney-sweepers come to dust"—is probably not the tone Shakespeare intended. I would like to ask Mr. Eliason, how do we know what tone to hear in Chaucer's poetry?

ELIASON   I can answer the question only obliquely—obliquely in this way—that I want to revert to something that has already been said. So far as tone is concerned, we readily grasp the very great difference in tone between the Miller's Tale and the Clerk's Tale—that's perfectly obvious. Now for subtleties and nuances of tone, there we have to do as best we can. What we have been doing in the past is what has been done a little bit this morning: we invoke this sophisticated audience of Chaucer's. How sophisticated were they? I've looked hard for evidence about it, and I've read what people have said about it. The sophistication of the audience is deduced from Chaucer's poetry. We don't actually know anything about the sophistication of that audience. We have one glimpse of the audience in that famous manuscript of *Troilus*, where Chaucer is depicted reading to an audience, and the most striking thing there is that half of them aren't paying attention at all and the other half are asleep![3] We constantly are reminding ourselves that, if we today fully appreciated the degree of sophistication the audience had, then we wouldn't even need to look for the signposts that Mr. Kaske is honest enough to insist should be present in Chaucer's poetry. We invoke this audience, but we don't know a thing about it. For nuances of meaning or tone I think we must rely upon what Chaucer himself says rather than upon what we suppose his audience may have been thinking or feeling.

DUNCAN   Since I invoked the audience, perhaps I should answer. But I will not attempt to answer except to remind Mr. Eliason that regarding the one illumination we have of Chaucer reading, presumably from the *Troilus and Criseyde*, we have to remember

3. Corpus Christi College, Cambridge, MS. 61. The well-known illumination to which Mr. Eliason is referring is reproduced in color to accompany Margaret Galway's article, "The 'Troilus' Frontispiece," *MLR*, XLIV (1949), 161–177. Also reproduced in *Gothic Painting*, "Great Centuries of Painting" Series (Lausanne: Skira, 1945), p. 164.

that the plastic arts, the art of painting, in particular miniature-making, have their relative position in development; and that given the art of the time, the faces probably couldn't have been otherwise than looking, staring off someplace, or maybe asleep. We shouldn't look to this miniature for a realistic illustration of an audience listening to the poem. The very fact that somebody found Chaucer's reading so striking as to use it as a subject for a miniature it seems to me is evidence that he *did—striking* evidence that he did—and that there was a strong knowledge of the fact that he did among court circles and among the people who were connected with court circles—that he did indeed read his poems aloud. And he could have educated his audience!

REISS Since the question did invoke Shakespeare, perhaps I might add, I wonder how many people sitting in the Globe Theater were counting images and noting thematic patterns as a play was being put on there.

QUESTION In the Marriage Group where Chaucer seems to be giving an attitude about sovereignty of the mates in marriage in different tales, I was wondering whether he is concerned here with his own attitude about marriage as it should have been. In one tale—well, the Wife of Bath's, for instance—she thinks that the woman has the sovereignty in marriage. In some of the others the man is the dominant character. In the Franklin's Tale it's more nearly equal, isn't it? And I was wondering if he was giving his own attitude. We think of him as a fairly objective writer. Was he giving an attitude that would be more nearly like the attitude we think of today as an equalitarian sort of marriage?

KASKE I suppose it's always a very tricky business trying to decide whether the governing theme of a particular work represents what the writer himself really thinks about life. I can conceive of a writer presenting something in a work which he himself doesn't quite personally agree with. And I think the problem is perhaps a little stickier when we're dealing with medieval literature. But, for whatever it's worth, yes, my hunch is that in the Franklin's Tale we probably have about what Chaucer thought marriage ought to be. That has to be a guess, because I know of no other way of taking hold of it.

QUESTION Professor Eliason mentioned that the Wife of Bath's Tale and *Troilus* and the Franklin's Tale all three give full treatment to "ordinary love." But then in his presentation he slighted the Franklin's Tale. I was wondering, do you think there is a difference there—either that it's not the same kind of treatment of ordinary love or that it's not really ordinary love? It seems that with Dorigen and Arveragus we have buck-passing, when she comes to him with her problem.

ELIASON I'm not sure I shouldn't pass the buck myself. No, I don't believe there is buck-passing. I think that in the Franklin's Tale Chaucer is concerned about love at a different stage in the game than he is in *Troilus*. I was very much pleased with Mr. Kaske's comment about Dorigen's "rash promise" as it has been foolishly called again and again in modern criticism. There isn't anything rash about her promise. It was a very nice gesture on her part. Mr. Kaske brought that out very clearly. It was in play; it was in kindness; it was in decency that she made the promise. My point in dealing very briefly with the Franklin's Tale was that critics have been very harsh with it, very severe with it—and here's one instance where they were. I'm afraid that's only a partial answer.

QUESTION I'd like to ask Professor Kaske if he finds irony in the Tale of the Franklin, in the description of him in the General Prologue, and in his own Prologue. It seems that if Chaucer does express an ideal view of marriage, he certainly doesn't know what an ideal parent is like. And I just wonder if there is a touch of irony that qualifies putting in the Franklin's mouth Chaucer's own idealistic views.

KASKE I think my answer to that will be in two parts, both speculative. First, I come more and more to the conclusion that Chaucer likes to put thematically meaningful stories into the mouths of tellers who are not always quite up to the stories they tell. I think this is true of the Knight's Tale. For whatever it's worth, I read the Knight's Tale as perhaps the philosophical cornerstone of the *Canterbury Tales*; but God knows, if you look at the Knight's comments, within his own tale, I think they are the comments of a man who is so much the gentleman that he is just a little tedious as a story teller. All these *occupationes* that he uses, in which he spends—what, I think at one point over a hundred lines telling you what he's not going to tell you, and this kind of thing, you remember; and all this marvelous flirting around with whether he should tell you how Emelye performed her lustral rites, you know, shall I or shall I not, "And yet it were a game to heeren al" and so on—I think these are all comments on the teller. And yet I don't think they vitiate the force of the Knight's Tale as a very strong and compelling expression of wisdom according to Boethius. This is how I read it. Well, I find the same kind of thing elsewhere in Chaucer. So, if the Franklin is presented as in some ways lacking as a person, I wouldn't find that necessarily in conflict with his telling a story that's meant to be taken straightforwardly. Now a few details: the big stumbling block I think in the portrait of him in the General Prologue is this "Epicurus owene sone" bit. He's Epicurus' own son, and you all know about Epicurus in the Middle Ages. And yet there's always the possibility of the playfully abusive epithet—the kind of thing that Langland seems so fond of doing—"Thanne loked vp a lunatik · a lene thing with-alle"⁴ Apparently this refers to the author himself—at least that's what I make of it. I think most people read it that way. Certainly he's not taking himself seriously as a lunatic. What I'm getting at is that there is such a thing as epithet (which if it were used straightforwardly would be fearfully insulting) used in a kind of jocular, playful way—like saying "you old scoundrel," this sort of thing, and everybody knows you're not seriously calling the man a scoundrel. Well, that is my hunch (and again it has to be hunch) for how we are to take "Epicurus owene sone." I think it's probably said with a grin. I take his remarks about the Squire later to be all part of what I suggested in my paper—that is, part of his tactful interruption of the tale. That would dispose of him as a parent, I suppose.

QUESTION   I believe that it's Donaldson in the preface to his edition of Chaucer's poetry who says something like this—the new readings of Chaucer we are getting now (and he is referring to those who read Chaucer allegorically, who interpret him allegorically) are so opposed to the older readings that we can't have

---

4. *Piers Plowman*, Prologue, B-text, 1. 123.

them both; we have to choose. I'd like to ask each of the panel members if he could give me his impressions briefly about what I am to tell my Chaucer students. Do they have to choose between one or the other approach, or can they both work somehow?

DUNCAN   This, which is an excellent question, might be a good one to end on, since it would give each one of our four panelists an opportunity to express himself.

ELIASON   I think one of the most instructive things to do is to go back and see how Chaucer was viewed in the past. And in the past the most instructive people, it seems to me, are those who actually lived when he did, or in the century immediately after, and on up into the sixteenth century. They knew a great deal about Chaucer. That is to say they understood him to some extent; they also understood why they admired him—and they admired him beyond anybody else in the language—and they have no comment whatever about this allegorical interpretation. If the sophisticated audience of Chaucer keeps being conjured up, then obviously his fifteenth-century admirers weren't part of it. Our present allegorical school is of recent vintage, from the 1920s on. It's conceivable that we today aren't the repositories of all wisdom.

REISS   I'll cite another old colleague of mine, who, responding to the exegetical view of Chaucer, said, "It's very interesting, but if I accepted it, I'd have to say that my forty years of teaching Chaucer have been wrong, and in vain. How can I do that?" This is a very human problem, I suppose, and I tried to tell the man, "Well, that's silly; not at all!" I find a great deal of interest, myself, in Kittredge, in Lowes—Donaldson himself has all sorts of good things to say about style, Chaucer's narrative technique, structure, whatnot. I think that the exegetical approach is dealing wholly with theme, with the essential meaning of the work—not the apparent meaning, but the essential meaning. I again don't see as necessary that it has to be, or one has to say, *this* and nothing else. One can talk about the *littera*, the *sensus*, the *sententia*. Why not?

KASKE   I think there has been a decided break between older views of Chaucer and the ones now, but I don't think that the essential difference is between a merely literal reading and an allegorical meaning. *That* I do believe is a red herring. So far as allegorical meanings go, I think they have to be assessed on their own terms, on their own value. Some of them have, I think, been fairly convincing. I think a great many more have not. But that's par for scholarship, isn't it? I mean there's always more crap written than there is good stuff. This is how it goes. But, as I was saying, I think the really significant break is not simply in the advent of a lot of exegetical criticism, but in the fact that we are now reading the texts closely, whereas earlier generations of scholars, I think, did not do this—at least not to such an extent. That's the difference. And I would explain that simply by saying, yes, we do have at our command today more effective techniques for the analysis of literature. Much as I admire the intellectual achievements and the general culture of the Middle Ages, I think that one thing they did not have, apparently at least as far as our records go, were effective techniques for the analysis and the communication of analysis of literary works. That does seem to me to be primarily a modern invention. So in that way I think essentially I'd have to say we're better than they were.

WIMSATT   I too would find no particular or necessary conflict between traditional interpretation and interpretation which with the use of exegetical materials often will make, or will assert, allegorical implications to the stories. I think that a very good example of a Chaucer tale that has been progressively clarified by the use of Christian materials is the Clerk's Tale. Sledd's essay "The Monsters and the Critics" indicated a direction in which criticism could reconcile the monstrous behaviour of the hero and heroine with reasonable behaviour. You have to take the analogies that are constantly asserted between Griselda and Mary and Job and Christ as helping to resolve the problems that we find there.[5] And we end up with a tale that is reasonable and that, I think, we can present to the students as being a fine example of Chaucerian art, rather than apologizing for this tale

5. James Sledd, "The *Clerk's Tale*: The Monsters and the Critics," *MP*, LI (1953–1954), 73–82. Several critics—among them Elizabeth Salter, John P. Mc-Call, and Bernard F. Huppé—have since pointed out more fully the role of the Christian analogies in making the story acceptable.

and saying, "Well, it fits in pretty well with the Marriage Group" or something of that sort.

DUNCAN   On that fine note of conciliation between the two camps, if we may express it that way, I think we shall end this discussion.

Afterword

Reading the four papers after a lapse of several months since hearing them during the symposium, I am again impressed, as I was then, by the wide-ranging variance among their approaches, the cogency of their arguments, each from its author's own well-articulated point of view, and the possibilities for further fruitful investigation and interpretative discussion which they open up. Together with Professor Provost's introduction, here included with them for the first time, and the transcript of the lively panel discussion which immediately followed their oral delivery, they furnish a rich and provocative commentary upon Chaucer as a poet of love.

Though written independently and without prior consultation among their authors, the four papers cohere remarkably well. Mr. Eliason's brief analysis of the kinds of love depicted in Chaucer's poetry in addition to the "ordinary" love which is the main concern of his paper—allegorical, courtly, philosophic, and Christian—conveniently provides, along with the introduction, an effective background against which the three succeeding papers can be perspectively viewed. Not that the writers are always of like opinion; the coherence is a more complex matter than mere agreement. In fact the range is from agreement to almost total disagreement: as when, for example, Mr. Reiss would, I think, agree with Mr. Eliason that the *Book of the Duchess* is an odd sort of elegy but insists, in contrast to him, that it is a poem about love, though parodic rather than direct. Mr. Wimsatt, disagreeing with both, sees in the Black Knight's recital of his experiences with the "faire White" a symbolic apotheosizing of John of Gaunt's dead wife Blanche and would thus, I suppose, transfer the *Book of the Duchess*, in Mr. Eliason's classification, from a poem of allegorical to one of Christian love. On the one hand there is essential agreement between Mr. Kaske and Mr. Wimsatt in the matter of the ironic overtones of the garden and of May's presence there in the Merchant's Tale; the former's thesis is buttressed and enriched by the latter's discussion of the Tale in relation to the

Canticles tradition in medieval Latin literature. On the other hand Mr. Reiss demonstrates the extent of his disagreement with Mr. Eliason's reading of the Knight's Tale only as a conventional romance of courtly love; granting that the Tale is that, he insists that Chaucer's narrative is shaped by other purposes as well. It is the range along the agreement–disagreement axis, as these instances illustrate, which lends vibrancy to the coherence among the four papers.

Mr. Eliason's case for Chaucer's preeminence as the poet of "ordinary" love is persuasively argued. One wonders if he would be willing to extend the instances of proof of that contention to include the ironic mode: for example the narrator's assumption of the taste and language of the Miller, in the matter of sexual love-play, in describing the physical allurements of John the carpenter's wife Alisoun. Or, for that matter, the vulgarly forthright language of the other Alisoun's account of her love affair with clerk Jankyn. And on the other end of the emotional scale— in social rank and sophistication as well as occasion—can we not say that the Black Knight's account of his arduous wooing and long-deferred winning of his lady, though cast in courtly terms, is nevertheless within the realm of the psychological reality of "ordinary" love?

Mr. Reiss's reading of Chaucer might be said to tend toward the subsuming of all of Chaucer's poems (for I am uncertain where he would want to draw the line) under Mr. Eliason's heading of Christian love. If the purpose consciously striven for in Chaucer's art was to depict the imperfect actual in order to inculcate the image of the Christian ideal perfect, one wonders why Chaucer never chose to say so. Instead, what he says at the end of the General Prologue and more particularly in the Miller's Prologue is that the artist's obligation is to tell a tale after a man as nearly as he can, to adapt the manner and the matter to the mood and the nature of the depicted narrator ("Crist spak hymself ful brode in hooly writ" [I, 739]; "this Millere . . . tolde his cherles tale in his manere" [I, 3167]). Chaucer is saying, I think, that as far as he as writer is concerned a profane love vision is a profane love vision and a churl's bawdy tale is a bawdy churl's tale. Such a conclusion is thoroughly in accord with his "retracciouns" appended to his address to the reader at the end of the Parson's Tale, wherein he beseeches his readers' prayers that

Christ forgive him his "enditings" of worldly vanities among which he includes specifically and by recognizable designation each and every one of the dream visions, the *Troilus* and the *Canterbury Tales*, "thilke that sownen into synne" (x, 1085). The only works besides the Parson's Tale he is willing to have his readers judge under Paul's rubric to Timothy: "Al that is writen is writen for oure doctrine"—partially quoting II Timothy 3:16— are his translation of Boethius and "othere bookes of legendes of seintes, and omelies, and moralitee, and devocioun" (x, 1087).

Now if a medieval reader, piously and doctrinally bent, chose to take Paul's words to Timothy, more accurately translated "All scripture is given, by inspiration of God and is profitable for doctrine ...," in a larger context to include all writings, even Chaucer's poems about life and love, he was, I suppose, free so to do. And then he might find in those poems ironic hints of the ideal adumbrated through the profane fictions. That he could successfully perform such a feat Mr. Reiss, who has made himself by his devoted studies a reasonable facsimile of the medieval reader, has competently demonstrated. But I would contend that the success of both the medieval reader and Mr. Reiss is due not primarily nor in most instances to Chaucer's deliberate and conscious intention (especially when he drops no hint) but rather to the closed intellectual, moral, and doctrinal environment in which both the medieval reader and Chaucer lived. To make this environment available to the modern reader is surely a legitimate function of criticism; and this I see as the chief value of Mr. Reiss's re-creation of Chaucer's parodies of love.

That Chaucer was a conscious artist, in this sense an intellectual poet, and, as far as his mature works are concerned, consciously in control of his material I suppose no critic would today seriously deny. A question can certainly be raised as to the exact point of division between his immature and his mature works—that is, at what point in the surviving canon, arranged as exactly as it is possible to do so in order of composition, he actually demonstrates that he is in artistic control. Opinions on this matter would vary, no doubt, though I suspect there would be fairly general agreement that the point comes about where he gets his ducks and other birds in a row (pun intended) in the *Parliament of Fowls*—a poem which might be considered Chaucer's contribution to the poetry of the sociology of love, if we may add to Mr. Eliason's categories. However firmly he is in control in the *Parliament*, a question still debated, it seems a legitimate expectation of criticism that more assured evidence of such control should be manifest in it than in the two poems which are generally conceded to have been written before it. In this regard the brief but telling characterization of the *Parliament* by Mr. Eliason seems to me to pinpoint quite precisely the evidence of its author's having been in control. And here I reveal the particulars of my agreement and disagreement with Mr. Eliason, who somewhat categorically, I feel, asserts the success of the *House of Fame* and the failure of the Knight's Tale. The former appeals to me not as a unified whole but rather as an untidy assemblage of fairly discordant parts, mainly registering youthful enthusiasm for the materials and craft of poetry, but not showing much control over either. That the latter is a failure considered in terms of its genre—courtly romance—and its teller—the naively philosophical knight who is yet experienced in the ways of his world—I cannot agree. I would insist, instead, that it is in its own way a successful poem about several kinds of love.

These remarks bring me to consideration of Mr. Kaske's paper on the Marriage Group. The marriage relationship, though it is not *sub nomine* included in Mr. Eliason's categories of love, is surely a legitimate field of concern to the love poet. And Chaucer makes the most of it in a considerable variety of its ramifications, as Mr. Kaske ably demonstrates. What especially reassures me about the demonstration is the unstated but nevertheless indisputable fact which emerges from Mr. Kaske's analyses of the four tales and the elaborate interplay of their mutual connections, parallelisms, and contrasts: namely that all is manifestly in keeping with an imaginative extension of Chaucer's stated intention, which was to "telle a tale after a man," or a woman, and not to tell it "untrewe." I cannot resist adding, even at the risk of riding my own hobbyhorse too obviously, that Chaucer's brilliant performance here is equally in keeping with and equally a logical and imaginative extension of the precepts he found inculcated in the rhetorical treatises of Geoffrey of Vinsauf.

Finally, and to return these scattered and doubtless opinionated observations to Chaucer as poet of love, I want to register my hearty appreciation of Mr. Wimsatt's valuable contribution to the topic. His paper provides a full and lucid account of how the medieval world received perhaps the greatest love poem in its inheritance from its past. In illustrating the subtleties of Chaucer's appropriation of the Canticles tradition to the exigencies of his art, Mr. Wimsatt demonstrates, what has been indeed the subject of all four papers, the nice distinctions with which Chaucer manipulates the ideas and the language of love.

Edgar H. Duncan

Index

DATE DUE